Praise for *Redefining Smart*

An urgent call for redefining educational outcomes and a compelling argument for personalization of education. Markham convincingly explains why education is much more than developing cognitive skills and proposes practical ways to cultivate what matters for life.

—Yong Zhao, Presidential Chair, Director
Institute of Global and Online Education
University of Oregon

"Choose courage, not fear." With these words Thom Markham begins his book Redefining Smart. *He offers a research-based educational vision for changing our definition for student success in the 21st century. The book goes further to offer practical advice, tools, and reflective questions to assist teachers in choosing to have courage to change their practice and students' lives.*

—Bob Lenz, Executive Director
Buck Institute for Education
CEO and Founder, Envision Schools

For over twenty years it's been known that intelligence is far more than one's IQ, and that a powerful relationship exists between the heart and brain that affects one's ability to self-regulate and navigate the complexities of life. By integrating the new science of heart intelligence into the conversation about deeper learning, inquiry, and 21st century skills, Thom Markham not only redefines intelligence, he shows that positive emotions hold the key to sustained optimal performance, sharper cognitive functioning, and the kind of heartfelt collaboration and mentoring that inspire young people to become resilient, capable, and open-minded adults. This book points the way to the future of education.

—Rollin McCraty, Director of Research
Institute of HeartMath
Boulder Creek, CA

In Redefining Smart, *Thom Markham makes an urgent call for school change that will resonate with anyone who entered the teaching profession because they care about children. Joyful learning that engages both heart and brain is not a squishy, feel-good idea. Nor is it in opposition to today's rigorous standards. Indeed, as Markham explains in detail, today's students will not be prepared to tackle the challenges ahead unless we help them learn to think, collaborate, communicate, and feel. Speaking directly—and respectfully—to teachers, he outlines practical steps to create the culture of inquiry that all children deserve.*

—Suzie Boss
Author of *Bringing Innovation to School,* and Edutopia blogger

Dr. Markham offers up smart research and fresh thinking about our most powerful and human way of teaching: inquiry. Written as short, accessible chapters with reflection questions to guide the experience, the overall effect of this multi-course experience is, not surprisingly, a wide smile and full heart. One of the most accessible, thoroughly researched and empowering books on the transformative power of inquiry-based teaching that I've ever read.

—Kimberly L. Mitchell, Founder and CEO
Inquiry Partners

It only took until 2015, but we finally have the book that provides the quintessential guide to 21st century learning. Redefining Smart *offers a simple, yet complex, road map to transform our students' educational experiences. While you read, throw out everything you think you know about determining students' abilities, focus on authentic learning over time, and visualize your schools and what they could (and should) be. The book is a call for change in our instructional practices, but clearly defines the Why? behind making these essential changes and the impact they will have on students. I cannot wait to put it in the hands of all my instructional leaders! Markham nailed it!*

—Rob Thornell, Assistant Superintendent
Northwest ISD
Fort Worth, TX

My work with Thom Markham began in 2005 as we embarked on a process of revising how learning looks at Olds High School. Teaching today requires personalization: connecting the heart and mind for both educators and learners; the fostering of personal rigor in project-based learning environments; and the ability to work in a team rather than a group. Thom has achieved in his book the same outcomes he achieves when working in schools face to face—that special ability to connect us to the sacred responsibility we have as educators in exposing our students to the skills they need. Markham has truly put his heart into the words of this book.

—Tom Christenson, Principal
Olds High School
Olds, Alberta CA

In a world that is struggling to figure out what 21st century teaching really means, Markham provides a clear path for moving forward. Redefining Smart *reaches beyond a compartmentalized view of lesson design and curriculum by creating an exciting imperative for a new rigor. Markham sets a vision for classrooms that build relationships, embrace emotions, develop academic mastery, and ensure that students graduate with the ability to communicate and collaborate. I can't wait to share* Redefining Smart *with our K–12 faculty.*

—Tim Fish, Associate Headmaster
McDonough School
Baltimore, MD

Redefining Smart *emphasizes the importance of unlocking a passion for learning within our students and guiding them to exercise their curiosity about the world inside of the classroom.*

Thom Markham provides resources, examples, and guided reflection questions to spark rich discussions about what it means to teach in the 21st century.

—Julie Helber, Principal
Saline High School
Saline, MI

This is a ground breaking book, and should be required for new and practicing teachers. Redefining Smart *effectively introduces educators to the world of self-directed learning through the lens of how we ourselves must change as educators. Markham has captured the essence of contemporary neuroscience, pedagogy, and cultural shifts and woven them into a cohesive and compelling image of who each of us could become if we redefine "smart."*

—Carol Spencer, Director of Curriculum
Addison Northwest Supervisory Union
Vergennes, VT

Thom Markham passionately engages all students in a positive manner using individualized inquiry-based learning techniques. He includes rigor and relevance as well as extensive research.

—Susan L. Harmon, Science and FACS Teacher
Neodesha Junior/Senior High School
Neodesha, KS

Every idea in this book is critical for educators—from the idea of a classroom functioning as an ecosystem, to addressing creativity, to encouraging and learning from failure, to the ideas of collaboration.

—Melissa Weatherwax, Elementary Teacher
Poestenkill Elementary School
Poestenkill, NY

In Redefining Smart, *Thom Markham reflects on the latest research in psychology, medicine, sociology, physics, social media, and business to articulate a clear vision for K–12 education. He synthesizes what we have learned in the past fifty years about human growth, productivity, and creativity to challenge educators at every level to break the mold of an outdated industrial paradigm and systematically rebuild the learning model for today's and tomorrow's students and world citizens. On every page he offers convincing evidence, cogent arguments, and actionable next steps for educators, parents, and community leaders who hear his clarion call for systemwide reinvention. This book should be read, discussed, argued about, and referenced by everyone who cares about our children enjoying full citizenship in an increasingly interconnected and dynamic global community. Put it on your short list of must-reads.*

—Frank Livoy, Associate Director
Delaware Center for Teacher Education
University of Delaware

Redefining Smart

*Awakening Students'
Power to Reimagine
Their World*

Thom Markham

CORWIN
A SAGE Company

FOR INFORMATION:

Corwin

A SAGE Company

2455 Teller Road

Thousand Oaks, California 91320

(800) 233-9936

www.corwin.com

SAGE Publications Ltd.

1 Oliver's Yard

55 City Road

London EC1Y 1SP

United Kingdom

SAGE Publications India Pvt. Ltd.

B 1/I 1 Mohan Cooperative Industrial Area

Mathura Road, New Delhi 110 044

India

SAGE Publications Asia-Pacific Pte. Ltd.

3 Church Street

#10-04 Samsung Hub

Singapore 049483

Printed in the United States of America

ISBN 978-1-4833-5896-3

Executive Editor: Arnis Burvikovs

Senior Associate Editor: Desirée A. Bartlett

Editorial Assistant: Andrew Olson

Production Editor: Amy Schroller

Copy Editor: Matthew Sullivan

Typesetter: C&M Digitals (P) Ltd.

Proofreader: Dennis W. Webb

Indexer: Molly Hall

Cover Designer: Karine Hovsepian

Marketing Manager: Kerry Garagliano

This book is printed on acid-free paper.

SFI® Certified Sourcing
www.sfiprogram.org
SFI-00453

15 16 17 18 19 10 9 8 7 6 5 4 3 2 1

Contents

Preface

Be the Change You Want to See

Or, Why This Book Is Different

CHOOSE COURAGE, NOT FEAR

Those four words may not seem like an adequate guide to becoming an inquiry-based teacher, but they form the foundation for the advice in this book. So much of what lies ahead in education requires choice, character, and conviction. This marks a shift for educators. Throughout the last 30 years or so, the solutions to the challenge of transforming education into a system capable of inspiring students to become skillful, creative, knowledgeable problem solvers fell into familiar territory: What types of curricula, standards, skills, strategies, and adaptations to classroom teaching methods will be necessary to pull even with the 21st century? This approach to change persists—and will for some time. But as education crosses the divide between a transmission model built on industrial rules and an inquiry model, the teacher's role changes dramatically.

The move from "Lord of the Board" to "Guide on the Side" has entered the educational lexicon, so the issue already is in view. When a teacher comes out from behind the lectern, leaves the front of the room, kneels beside a student to coach him or her through a problem, offers feedback designed to promote confidence and perseverance, and becomes a true partner in the learning process, the relationship between teacher and student automatically shifts. It's no longer about *telling;* it's about listening, observing, and creating the channel of trust that opens up a personal connection between two individuals.

WHY PERSONALITY MATTERS

The basics of good coaching can be learned, especially if it's aimed at helping a student master a math problem, write a better essay, or give a more polished presentation. In fact, if that's all the inquiry-based system of the future was expected to do, a natural evolution of teacher skill sets would easily take place, reinforced by a new course requirement in every credential program designed to teach effective coaching techniques.

By itself, this would be a valuable step. In Chapters 7 and 8 on coaching, these techniques will be explored in detail. However, the future tells us that technique will be necessary, but not sufficient. Collaborative inquiry in pursuit of deeper learning, creativity, design thinking, and critical inquiry succeeds when fueled by persistence, resiliency, curiosity, and other intangible personal assets that can be elicited, but not easily taught.

The emergence of those assets (or, as I will term them, *intelligent behaviors*) relies on establishing a coherent, caring relationship with students—a bond that science is now beginning to reveal as deeply non-verbal and calibrated by the relationship between teacher and student. Sincere care, authentic communication, and an orientation to potential rather than problems shift thinking, affect clarity, and stimulate imagination. The brain changes, and behavior follows.

The connecting link is emotion. For this reason alone, we must reengage education and emotions. Experts usually cite technology and the shifting nature of knowledge as core drivers for a new model of education. But those changes simply surface the deeper challenge. As young people focus less on recall and regurgitating information, they have to get better at solving problems, asking questions, making critical judgments, and persisting at finding solutions—the staples of inquiry. Those qualities can't be directly taught; instead, they draw from a deeper well of personality attributes intimately tied to emotional life.

Fortunately, there is a grand shift underway in our understanding of emotions, with deep implications for helping young people become creative, resilient individuals. Emotions communicate, and when sitting beside a student in an inquiry-based classroom, personality matters a great deal. As you might guess, not just any personality, but one focused on the positive side of life. Thus, the further we advance into the 21st century, the more the personality traits of the teacher will matter. Rather than the usual focus—what subjects are taught, what's the latest and best strategy, or which textbook or curriculum has been adopted this year—educational planners and administrators will ask, *How do we identify, attract, nurture, and train teachers who have an inquiry-friendly personality?*

THE PERSONAL JOURNEY

For you, however, the reader of this book, I will pose the question differently. The very word *trainer* needs to be removed from your vocabulary. No amount of passive listening, in the form of stand-in-front-of-the-room-and-talk-at-you workshops, will fill the inquiry-based skills gap. Nor will the latest initiative or program adopted by your district provide you more than a vague road map. And no book, this one included, can provide more than a starting point of ideas, tips, and useful information.

In some ways, this is not news. All of us know, either as students or from our experience as teachers, that the ultimate skill of teaching is driven by personality. Search your own history in school and recall the teacher who mattered most to you. Usually, a smiling face pops into view—someone who cared or took time with you. Or, just as often, it's a teacher who taught you important knowledge, but conveyed it with a passion and sense of wonder that lit that same flame within you.

But it's time to make this a new standard for effective teaching, not an irregular occurrence. Inquiry draws on deeper aspects of self—from both student and teacher—than has been customary in the past. Using personality and positive relationships to drive learning is now central to education.

The primary lesson is hard, but essential: Education doesn't qualify any longer as a *thing*. You don't lob information at students like a beach ball and hope they bat it back. Instead of a transitive verb with an object, to *learn* denotes a process of engaging a vast flow of information, with teachers giving that flow of facts and concepts meaning and purpose through connected dialogue. The process mandates a critical connection between you and the learner—and relationships always put the psyche in play. In the same way that employees in high-performing industries are urged to reflect inwardly and develop an agile, communicative, collaborative, and creative self as a means to work with and influence others, you will need to do similar internal research. To become a future-ready teacher, the conversation turns personal, increasingly spun more in the direction of Gandhi: How do you be the change you wish to see? The shift requires emotional balance and attention to personality factors that enhance or diminish relationships and attitudes. It refocuses professional growth onto the self rather than improved methods for delivering information.

DEVELOPING YOUR INQUIRY-BASED SKILL SET: WHAT YOU CAN EXPECT FROM THIS BOOK

Now, for some frank admissions. No one is an expert on a system that has not yet been invented. The blue-collar philosopher Eric Hoffer said it well over 60 years ago: "In a time of drastic change it is the learners who inherit the future. The learned usually find themselves equipped to live in a world that no longer exists."

So welcome to the club in a time of drastic change. As temporary leader of the club for next 180 pages or so, I will offer practical advice for teachers of all grade levels (and professors!) that follows a logical pattern. However, if you are used to reading educational books that begin with strategies, it may not feel so logical. I believe that a *mindshift* is necessary—a leap in imaginative powers that pushes us past conventional boundaries and beliefs about intelligence and emotions. So I'll start there. From that point, I'll move on to Monday morning and ways to implement the vision of teaching students to be smarter in ways more consistent with 21st century life.

Overall, here is what to expect from the book—and what I believe is necessary to craft an inquiry-based skill set.

- *Learn why your attitude matters.* I'll start with reflections on the evolutionary trends of the world today. I promise nothing too deep or philosophical, but the inquiry-based direction for education is no accident; it's fueled by core shifts in technology and demand information, forcing us to move from recall and retention to application and creativity. How we support the deeper learning necessary in this environment is the challenge, but one powerful trend stands out: increasing evidence from positive psychology and neuroscience demonstrating that *care* and *connectivity* affect brain function and emotional readiness. That's the key research link showing us how teacher personality and an inquiry-based ecosystem activate higher order thinking and intelligent behaviors—and it is a theme underlying every chapter.
- *Rethink intelligence.* If we want young people to think and behave in ways that help them succeed in today's world, then I believe we have to let go of old notions of intelligence that focus exclusively on cognitive achievement. The 21st century requires a new mental model of "smart" that integrates emotions, intellect, and culture—and helps us understand how to set up the right conditions for critical thinking, persistence, resilience, curiosity, and empathy to flourish.

- *Know the tools of inquiry.* From there, in Chapters 5 through 10, I'll introduce the tools that make up an inquiry-based skill set. These include tools for thinking, methods for giving learning a powerful context (a necessity in an inquiry-based classroom), insights into eliciting creativity from students, and tools for making teamwork and collaboration the norm in school. During these chapters, I'll refer often to the Common Core State Standards. The new standards, regardless of how many states adopt them or if they fade with time, grow out of the shared recognition that problem solving and application trump retention and recall in the new world. They will be a useful guide. But our goal will be to learn how to "teach above the standards"—a terrific phrase that a very enthusiastic and thoughtful middle school teacher shared with me recently.
- *Contribute to the conversation.* A solid, enduring, high-quality, inquiry-based educational system that serves the needs of global youth in a challenging world will not be built by a team of experts. It will be created and crafted by an assembly of caring educators, perhaps 10 million strong, who offer a constant stream of ideas and insights through the digital biosphere. That's the million-teacher march that's required, and the ranks are forming. Join in. In the Appendix, I'll provide links, addresses, and sites. It's time to get active.

Finally, I'll work hard to keep this book light. This matter of inquiry is too serious to be constantly frowning, besides which the research tells us that when we frown, our brain starts to think in terms of survival instead of a joyful future. Keep smiling.

Publisher's Acknowledgments

Corwin gratefully acknowledges the contributions of the following reviewers:

Melissa Miller
Science/History Instructor
Randall G. Lynch Middle School
Farmington, AR

Lisa Graham
NBCT, Director, Special Education
Berkeley Unified School District
Berkeley, CA

David Vernot
Curriculum Consultant
Hamilton, OH

Melissa Weatherwax
Elementary Teacher
Poestenkill Elementary
Poestenkill, NY

About the Author

 **Thom Markham** is a psychologist, author, speaker, educator, thought leader, and internationally recognized consultant to schools and districts focused on project-based inquiry, 21st century skills, innovation, school redesign, and student empowerment. As founder and CEO of PBL Global, he has worked with over 250 schools and districts, and conducted workshops for nearly 6,000 teachers across five continents, providing proven methods and resources for designing high-quality, challenging, and authentic projects. His previous books include several best-selling books on project-based learning, including the *Project Based Learning Design and Coaching Guide: Expert Tools for Innovation and Inquiry for K–12 Educators,* as well as numerous articles on school transformation. He can be contacted through his website, www.thommarkham.com.

Part I

Making Children Smarter

1 Be Future-Ready

Entering a Relationship-Driven World

During my days as a classroom teacher, I occasionally received a directive from the principal sending me down to the district office to review applications submitted by prospective teachers applying for a position. My job was to weigh in with my rating on whether they should be considered for an interview.

The files were hefty—some nearly an inch thick—and padded by an assortment of boilerplate letters of recommendation, classroom observations noted on standardized forms, college courses and degrees, and the prized document: the teaching certificate that qualified the applicant to step in the classroom and improve the minds of students.

Of course, the documents revealed quickly who was minimally qualified to teach, and who wasn't. But the files told me nothing about the personality of the teacher, the dreams and aspirations of the candidate, or those intangibles that separate a great teacher who inspires from one who merely fulfills the duties of the profession.

And it didn't matter.

Why? The underlying presumption was that every certificated teacher possessed identical skills. New teachers could be slotted in for old ones. Rookies could sharpen their skills and become veterans, but be expected to do the sharpening by expanding their ability to deliver the product, whether it was the latest pedagogical program for reading or a new system for behavior management.

Of course, a teaching credential doesn't guarantee competence, and performance varied in the classroom. But the hiring process mirrored the demands of the factory model. If students remain in rows, intent on obtaining a standardized education and focused on information alone, the skill set of the teacher is pretty straightforward: Broadcast the right content, with a few questions sprinkled into the delivery, while managing the classroom for maximum impact and retention. Students behave or else receive a reprimand or referral slip. Students who can't control their "bad" emotions suffer consequences.

While there are still too many front-of-the-room teachers, the model is changing, I know. Most teachers know the best practices for engaging students in learning. But the old view of emotions persists—and that, I believe, is about to change radically. A future-ready teacher recognizes that emotions are an ally, not a handicap.

RETHINKING EMOTIONS

An old joke, retold many times, goes like this: A person claims to be able to break an egg, scramble it, and reassemble it into its original form. How? *Easy.* Feed it to a hen.

Describing how emotions develop and cohere into a successful, intelligent person resembles the egg joke. Think of friends or colleagues who radiate warmth, awareness, presence, empathy, openness, curiosity, quickness, a light touch to life, a sixth sense kind of ability to connect with others, or other obvious signs of brightness. How did they get that way? The process through which people become personable, capable, and heartfelt beings—a reasonable definition of a *whole* person—is still mysterious. No wonder eggs symbolize creation.

Ten years ago, personality theorists traced the root cause of emotions to fixed traits—a kind of win–lose genetic lottery, with odds affected by early upbringing. The same held true for your emotional intelligence (EQ), which most academic psychologists considered just another language to describe personality. In other words, not much actionable news if someone wanted to know how to become more emotionally literate.

There was a further problem. Generally, emotions equate to unhappiness. Asked about emotions, likely you visualize tears, dysfunction, wild behavior, or other signs that life has gone off the rails. This view is tied to an *ungovernable* dimension associated with emotions—the sense that they come and go according to their private timetable—which affects how they are viewed in the classroom: If students get their emotions under control, they can learn.

It's altogether natural, then, that emotions have been studied to death. That's a pun, because the overwhelming weight of scientific literature focuses on negative emotions—the kind that eventually wear you out and leave you debilitated or dead.

In a famous quote, often repeated, George Vaillant, a research psychiatrist at Harvard University, noted in 2008 in *Spiritual Evolution* that out of a half a million lines, the leading American text, *The Comprehensive Textbook of Psychiatry,* "devotes 100 to 600 lines each to shame, guilt, terrorism, anger, hate, and sin; thousands of lines to depression and anxiety, but only five lines to hope, one line to joy, and not a single line to faith, compassion and forgiveness" (p. 22).

This omission is key to understanding how inquiry can fail, or will succeed, in the future, but first let's examine the reason behind the scientific bias. Partly, negative emotions can be easily studied by instruments. In response to threat, disappointment, and general unpleasantness fear and worry activate stress circuits in the body. Adrenal glands pump out cortisol, the hind brain lights up (the site of fear or flight response), the mouth dries up, the lips curl, and so on. Even with a small slight in personal relationships, fingertip temperatures drop, a reaction to feeling left out that a simple thermometer can measure.

But in the end, the chief culprit is history. Focusing on negativity, and fixing it, fits nicely with the image of the club-wielding ancestor and the dominant view of human nature derived from primitive times: more competitive rather than cooperative; more self-serving than altruistic; and more focused on self-preservation than on the needs of others. Stoked for over 200 years by Darwinism, behaviorists, and reductionists, this is the *deficit* view of human nature.

Where has this model led us? In education, it means we dissect children by separating out emotions (bad) from the brain (good). Academic learning is distinguished from social-emotional learning, as if brain and the rest of the body operate in isolation. The brain itself gets divided into forebrain, hindbrain, mammalian brain, limbic system, and so on, furthering the mistaken assumption that the brain performs its miracles through isolated modules. A steady diet of units, pacing guides, and curriculum strategies reinforces this skewed view by taking a narrow aim at stimulating a child's cognitive apparatus rather than his or her inner life.

In an inquiry-based system, the model fails. The capacity and engagement required for students to be successful in an inquiry-based system grows out of a positive attitude, optimism, the capacity to see failure as a form of helpful feedback, purposeful actions, a growth mindset, and the ability to harness emotions to power up learning, not get in the way. That's the definition of today's lifelong learner. It also leads to one conclusion: Inquiry won't happen without a whole-child vision to guide education. For a 21st century educational system, validating the inner life of a child and activating the personal assets of a child are core outcomes. If we can't figure out a system to make it happen, we're in trouble.

EMOTIONS AS ALLIES

Now, for the courage part. Readers paying close attention will note that industrial education and the deficit model reinforce one another. For example, the old view of emotions reinforces the split between academic learning and social-emotional learning, as if one system were designed for thinking and the other for coping with stress or challenge. It also means that cognition reigns in schools, reinforced by almost daily neuroscientific reports that tout the amazing powers of the brain, but omit any mention of emotions.

Beyond the fact that good science tells us that the body and brain are partners in a complex dance of thinking and emotions, viewing emotions as absent or negative won't work in an inquiry-based system. This makes it hard on inquiry-based teachers, who face charges that they lack rigor or focus too much on "soft" skills. But a more refined view makes clear that soft skills such as communicating effectively are really the "hard" skills of life; they require emotional balance and deep attention to emotional development. This is the message education is receiving from industry and the broader work world.

It will be helpful to be armed with data. The conversation about emotions began to change five decades ago, when psychologists began to ask, What would happen if we studied what is right with people? The question had the same ripple effect as the butterfly that can influence the weather on the other side of the globe by simply flapping its wings: it led to the monsoon of positive psychology, the scientific and practical study of optimal functioning.

Positive psychology is its own discipline, a field with measures and diagnostic models aimed at understanding the strengths and virtues that enable individuals and communities to thrive. For example, the Positive Psychology Center at the University of Pennsylvania promotes research into the human capacity for love and work, courage, compassion, resilience, creativity, curiosity, integrity, self-knowledge, moderation, self-control, and wisdom. The goal of the center is to quantify the effects of joy, purpose, contentment, and love, or to discover how positive emotions, such as optimism, hope, self-efficacy, creativity, gratitude, humor, and empathy, promote well-being and affect the expression of one's intelligence (www.positivepsychology.org; see also Seligman, 1991).

That last point is critical for our purposes. Can children really get smarter, in a deeper sense, if they grow up as flourishing individuals? That's the premise of positive psychology. Using positive strengths as a foundation results in young people discovering their purpose and goals—the essentials for engagement and achievement in school.

The renewed emphasis on optimal human functioning is creating new metrics for human performance, to the extent that it's difficult to distinguish the goals of positive psychology from everyday culture. Positivity, health,

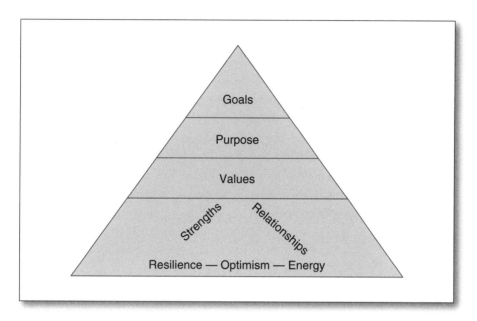

and well-being reach into daily life, corporate values, productivity and communication training, relationship counseling, addictive behavior therapies, and exercises designed to improve concentration, expand our moral compass, access creativity, or expand job skills—everywhere, in fact, but schools.

What Does It Mean to "Redefine Smart"?

Obviously, I'm not agnostic on the subject of positive psychology. And I don't expect teachers to become experts. But I believe strongly that educators will need to breach the defenses of the battalions of advocates invested in negative emotions if we want inquiry to succeed. The title of this book is *Redefining Smart*. Smart, in ways that all of us are trying to figure out, now means a mix of academic mastery, intellectual capacity, and a skillful life rooted in the ability to collaborate and communicate ideas. Underlying the inquiry-based approach is a strong desire to help young people become *wholly* prepared for 21st century life by integrating thinking, doing, and feeling.

That's where positive psychology helps. For example, Barbara Fredrickson of the University of North Carolina, author of *Positivity* (2009), produced data showing that positive emotions had an "undo" effect, meaning that positive emotions counter the physiological effects of sadness and signal greater resilience. After a thorough study of evolutionary theory, she concluded that positive emotions built an individual's capacity for survival, every bit as important as fight or flight, but with a different purpose: to allow, over a longer time span, for the development of alliances, cooperative behaviors, and new skills. The enhanced resources built through positive emotions then increased the chances for health and fulfillment—an "upward spiral" that set civilization on trajectories of growth by promoting positive emotions and enabling the more expansive mindset necessary for growth.

Fredrickson came to call this the "broaden and build" theory, and proposed that a positive loop existed between positive emotions that allows people to live more fulfilling lives and perform better in life.

Studies confirm the broaden and build model, with optimism proving to be protective against disease and poor health, and to improve emotional vitality and satisfaction with life. The effects, I want to make clear, are physiological. Positive emotions, in the words of a leading scientist, provide "restorative biology" for people.

TEACHERS AS BRAIN CHANGERS

There's no agreed-on name for the new scientific model that will drive education (and most of the rest of society) into the future. But I'll use the term *connectionist model.*

That connections between people yield verifiable results is indisputable, as demonstrated by Carol Dweck's (2008) work on inducing a growth mindset in students and showing that measurable upward shifts in IQ occur when teachers unlimit their own expectations for performance. There's also well-validated research showing that brains exchange information, using mirror neurons to reflect interaction between people. In *Social Intelligence,* Daniel Goleman (2006), author of *Emotional Intelligence,* points out that neuroscience confirms that the brain is a dynamic organ wired for sociability, able to restructure its synapses and open needed pathways in milliseconds.

To use Goleman's term, intelligence reflects a "neural ballet," a fluctuating state that connects our brain to those around us. The richness of our interactions, our degree of social isolation, or the extent of daily stress triggers a cascade of hormones, immune reactions, and emotional responses that affect our thinking each moment of the day. Recent experiments even indicate that genes express differently in positive versus negative environments, connecting into different combinations based on input from surroundings. (It's worth reminding ourselves that each of those 100 million neurons in the brain has its own six feet of DNA, so we're talking about affecting brain development here.)

Rewiring the Brain

The connectionist model—a science that brings relationships, attitude, emotions, and brain functions into one understandable ecological whole—begins with neuroplasticity, the study of how experience changes the brain.

Using four major mechanisms (increasing neurons, altering synaptic connections between neurons, deepening the myelin sheath that governs connection speeds between neurons, and rearranging gene expression of individual neurons), the brain can lay down a new neural track in milliseconds, adapt to the needs and demands of the moment, and open up pathways that range from fear and flight to creative genius. With practice and repetition, the tracks endure. That's called learning.

During the Decade of the Brain in the 1990s, neuroscientists confirmed this revolutionary view of the brain. It's a dynamic, not a static, organ. Assumptions about the hardwired nature of the brain, or finite numbers of neurons, or fixed intelligence—all are now outdated. The brain responds to novelty, grows and grooves, and reflects the needs of its owner.

With the fundamental recognition that the brain is deeply social, it's becoming clear that emotional messages exchanged between people affect the physiological processes and biological structures of the brain and body. Further, and that a kind of behavioral synchrony or embodied rapport causes shifts in neural networks, frontal lobe functioning, and stress levels (Vacharkulksemsek & Fredrickson, 2012).

This research will be critical to the inquiry-based teacher's ability to engage students, as advocates for this new science make clear. Moreover, the research provides an important counterweight to a narrow cognitive or modular view of the brain, which underlies the testing approach. So I advocate knowing a bit more about the direction of brain science. A thumbnail: the brain is very active and very social.

The Social Brain

Dr. Dan Siegel (2012), for example, clinical professor of psychiatry at the University of California, Los Angeles, author of *Brainstorm* (a book about parenting and the brain), and a leading researcher in the field of interpersonal neurobiology, sees the brain as embedded in a social network, affected by information and energy that streams in from the environment, including the patterns of information and energy exchanged between people. Thus, relationships affect the brain directly. "When we get connected to other people," Dr. Siegel states, "We're shaping each other's minds."

An important fact here: the brain can be shaped by positive or negative experiences. Dr. Norman Doidge (2012), author of *The Brain That Changes Itself,* adds this dark note on plasticity: "While the main message of [the book] is that the human brain is far, far more resilient than most people ever imagined, especially in response to injury and illness, it's also far more vulnerable than we imagined in so far as the brain can be changed by experiences—for better or for worse." Investigators also note a "negativity bias" in the brain, perhaps a result of evolutionary adaptation to threat and the need for survival. For example, Dr. Rick Hanson (2012), author of *Buddha's Brain: The Practical Neuroscience of Love, Happiness, and Wisdom,* says about the brain and negativity: "This [bias] helped our ancestors survive, and it's very good at learning from bad experiences, but it's very bad at learning from good experiences."

In a highly personalized classroom, in which teachers coach students through the inquiry process, what will we put in students' brains, and to what effect? That's a fundamental question that inquiry-based teachers must ask—and answer. Again, I'll invoke the mantra of evidence-based education. The evidence is indisputable that positive relationships open a closed mind or rebuild the brain when it's been damaged by trauma. And the mechanisms have largely been identified.

I'll quote Dr. Louis Cozolino (2012), professor of psychology at Pepperdine University in Los Angeles and author of *The Social Neuroscience of Education,* who describes the biochemistry of a positive, loving interaction:

> We know that when people have positive emotional connections with each other, they have higher levels of serotonin, dopamine, and oxytocin. All of these different biochemicals down regulate anxiety. [They] regulate cortisol production, enhance neuroplasticity, and make for healthier learning systems. It's not just a nice Los Angeles Fufu idea. We have the mechanism of the action—we can see the result of their power. For example, how does love get translated into psychological health and learning and well-being? We know that now. It's not theology or philosophy anymore.

The reverse is equally true, of course. The higher the number of stressful interactions, the higher the levels of stress hormones in the brain, particularly cortisol. Cortisol inhibits protein synthesis, preventing neurons from creating new branches. It leads to hyper-activation of parts of the brain central to attention or shrinks parts of the brain critical to learning.

Inevitably, teacher relationships with students now include a therapeutic element, especially in classrooms with students who have endured high levels of trauma through poverty, neglect, or violence. I know that can be a foreign concept to very traditional educators. I once had a high school English teacher ask indignantly on the morning of the first day of a two-day workshop, "What? We're supposed to be counselors now?" He didn't return for day two, so I couldn't explain to him, "Yes, the skill set of a professional teacher has changed. Welcome to 21st century education."

POWERING UP YOUR PERSONALITY

You may have had an experience like mine: A new acquaintance at a gathering talked non-stop at me for 20 minutes, asked no questions about my life, and soon departed with a perfunctory smile. Later, I received feedback from a friend who also attended, who remarked that my new acquaintance thought I was "the smartest person he had met that day." (My opinion of him was the exact opposite.) The formula he used for that calculation was simple: He talked, and I listened. I was "smart" enough to stay focused on his concerns, though with his non-stop delivery, I hardly had a choice. No matter.

When people fail to connect, they don't seem smart to us—for good reason. Emotions send signals to your body—and your body responds in kind. Emotions such as joy or contentment correlate with increased frequency of genuine smiles known as Duchenne smiles. These smiles, named after a French neurologist from the 1800s, who also discovered muscular dystrophy, activate cheek muscles and crinkle the eyes to show sincere intention.

With enough practice, genuine smiles can be faked, so beware. But *faux* fails for other reasons as well. Duchenne smiles forecast increased attentional flexibility and better decision making, giving you a kind of window into someone else's brain. Plus, if you're smiling sincerely, you're probably thinking clearly yourself—and you can figure out who's your friend and who isn't. Smiling just doesn't open the face; it also opens the mind.

This is a literal fact, not a tired metaphor. When experiencing positive emotions, people expand their circle of trust, feel more inclusive, and expand their perspectives on the actions of someone else, leading to greater empathy and acceptance. In the presence of positive emotions, the own-race bias (the unconscious reaction to ethnic differences) disappears. Your body also experiences a biological shift—and so does the other person.

Now let's return to the argument in favor of positive emotions. It is becoming increasingly obvious that, while inquiry may be partly a solitary act, *no one learns alone.* Learning takes place within a larger context of information flow, interconnectivity, and global networks. It's nearly impossible to decipher what you know from what you learned from someone else. Further, science yields increasing evidence that *emotional* interconnectivity runs deeper than we imagined both within us and between us. The old view, that humans are separate from their environment or that physiological processes occur independent of surroundings, is obsolete.

Instead, there's evidence that humans function as part of an ecosystem in which positive emotional interactions lead to maximum growth. Moreover, the positive emotions that support greater resiliency and growth—the "upward spiral" described previously—are communicated through an attitude of openness, care, and sincere appreciation.

The lesson? Relationships don't just matter; in the emerging inquiry model, they function as the critical connector that determines the health of the ecosystem and the success of its members. The tenor of that connection is defined by warmth and positive expectations (not to be confused with the present jargon of high expectations for every student). Positive expectations begin with unconditional acceptance of every student, as well as holding a vision for their growth.

Teaching as Co-Learning

I propose that inquiry-based teachers, beyond seeing students (and ourselves) as whole beings and acknowledging emotions as critical to learning, will benefit from assuming a relationship-driven world is the new norm. This invites a drastic shift in the teacher–student relationship, from one of front-of-the-room expert to a mentor and partner in the learning process. Inquiry, in fact, is a *co-learning* process. Jeremy Rifkin (2014), the economist and futurist, puts it this way in his latest book:

> In the Collaborative Age, students will come to think of knowledge as a shared experience among a community of peers. Students learn together as a cohort in a shared-knowledge community. The teacher acts as a guide, setting up inquiries and allowing students to work in small-group environments. The goal is to stimulate collaborative creativity, the kind young people experience when engaged in many of the social spaces of the Internet. The shift from hierarchal power, lodged in the hands of the teacher, to lateral power, established across a learning community, is tantamount to a revolution in pedagogy.

Rifkin's view suggests that interconnectivity may lead to a surge in global creativity and unified purpose as the whole begins to respond to the challenges of the times. It also has immediate ramifications for teachers in inquiry-based environments. The old model of the isolated teacher, responsible for a slice of knowledge, or even the boss–worker hierarchy, won't stand much longer.

Instead, teaching becomes a communal enterprise. Teacher collaboration, professional learning communities, networking with colleagues, understanding schools as systems, student-centered learning—all these become part of an intentional method for collective effort. The future-ready teacher prepares the ground for students as well. Collaboration becomes a staple of the learning process, not just to teach the skill of teamwork, but also to invite students into the larger process of purposeful interconnectivity by supporting the *future of smart*. That's a term I'll resurrect in Chapter 10, where you will read that the relationship-driven world may go deeper than any of us imagine.

Beyond Self-Esteem

Finally, I'll note that, though no agreement exists among psychologists about what constitutes a positive emotion, it's not about happiness or some kind of wish-fulfilled self-esteem. Instead, certain universals usually make a top 10 list. Fredrickson's list includes joy, gratitude, serenity, interest, hope, pride, amusement, inspiration, awe, and love. For the last item, love, Fredrickson and other researchers reserve special comment, as do I. With its complexity and range, love encompasses other positive emotions. More to the point—and deepening the mystery of how emotions affect physiology—love packs more punch. It "out-powers" other emotions in its ability to heal and nurture the body, as well as influence the brain.

This opens the door to a critical area of understanding for the inquiry-based teacher. Normal science assumes that either we think or we feel. Science analyzes cognition and emotion as separate domains, with various scientific disciplines shifting between one perspective and the other. This has consequences for learning. Artificial intelligence theorists follow the egg approach: they dream of reassembling the components of intelligence into a highly functional machine. The psychiatric and pharmaceutical community searches for pills that suppress anxious emotions and leave the mind the space it needs for effective problem solving. Brain scientists seek the Holy Grail, the evidence that joy, sadness, and the ability to fill in the *New York Times* crossword all represent neurochemical bursts from neural networks.

Inquiry-based teachers will benefit from marching in the opposite direction. Intelligence is a more fluid, dynamic process than science previously believed. Neural plasticity and genetic research open the door to understanding how the 100 million neurons in your brain and the six feet of DNA in each of the 75 trillion cells in your body adapt, respond, and mold themselves to your needs. Right now, science classifies you as labile, mobile, and full of possibility. So the questions arise: How can we do the same for students? How do we help them get smarter?

To begin, there's no silver bullet. Intelligence is too complicated for that. But we'll proceed through the remainder of the book on the premise that a positive orientation to life opens the door to deeper learning in your students, helping them activate a higher percentage of those 100 million neurons in service to problem solving. All journeys require a "true north." That's ours.

Moving Forward . . .

Teaching as a Personal Journey

Shifting your focus as a teacher from professional development to personal development may feel unfamiliar. There are three simple, powerful steps that you can take, however, to begin the process:

1. ***Reflect on your beliefs, strengths, and challenges as a teacher.*** Confucius, one of history's early master teachers, said this about reflection: "By three methods we may learn wisdom: first, by reflection, which is noblest; second, by imitation, which is easiest; and third, by experience, which is the most bitter." So I recommend starting with the noble route by taking inventory of your beliefs and seeking out any inner roadblocks that keep you from a whole-hearted connection with your students. Ask yourself, "How positive am I?" Or: "Do I really believe that I can help young people grow and change dramatically?" Or: "Who inspires me?" Keep the focus on you, not your students. In fact, ask yourself *any* question that's on your mind about teaching. Start there, and see where it leads.

2. ***Draft a Personal Mission Statement to commit to action.*** Reflection without action doesn't achieve much. Also, the science of connection is closely related to *intention*. Your intentions and beliefs, for example, can push up the IQ scores of your students. Crafting a Personal Mission Statement is a great way to give yourself a North Star in life, both personally and professionally (and you've chosen a profession in which your two lives can't be separated). The statement can be brief or long, accompanied by photos or drawings or a separate one-line credo. It doesn't matter. What do you stand for? What guides you? What is your personal "constitution"? I'm going to suggest that you write it down, sign it, and post it. But first, make a draft or two, and then take Step 3.

3. ***Create a cohort.*** Life is much easier with a friend, and teaching can be lonely. It's been estimated that teachers make 70 decisions an hour. How do you share all that? Not easy, so I suggest you organize it. First, convince one or two of your teaching colleagues to read the book along with you. Periodically, check in with your "book club." What do you like about what you're reading? What do you question (yes, it's inevitable) in the book? Most important, what can you add to the conversation about inquiry? If you like to journal, or jot notes on your laptop, all the better. At the end of the book, you will have a set of rich observations that will make you a more skilled inquiry-based teacher. And then: Write your final Personal Mission Statement.

Reflection Questions . . .

1. Does the information on emotions surprise you? In what way?

2. What examples can you remember in your own teaching or learning in which relationships made a difference to your students or yourself?

3. What steps can you take to be happier—and would that change your teaching?

2 Let Go of IQ
Why Beliefs Limit Intelligence

I received my first (and most unforgettable) lesson in intelligence from a student enrolled in a class full of what I termed artists, rebels, and misfits. It was a special intervention and support class designed to discourage students from transferring to the alternative school or dropping out. Included in this group, as a sort of flag bearer, was a boy I will call Cory, a big, tough 15-year-old with a keen look in his eye. I liked him immediately, but he had a reputation that was probably deserved. If there was a fight in the hallway, Cory was usually there—and he seemed to have something to do with it. The assistant principal never could gain a conviction, though. Somewhere back in elementary school, Cory had mastered plausible denial.

In his first year of high school, when I met him, Cory failed nearly every class, and by his sophomore year, he was completely disengaged. However, in the middle of 10th grade, something caught my eye: Cory always carried a wad of cash in his pocket, usually amounting to more than a hundred dollars. The assistant principal said it was drug money. But I asked Cory about it one day, and he had a surprising explanation: He was the acclaimed master mechanic in his neighborhood. He fixed cars and motorcycles for friends and neighbors—and they paid him in cash.

As the year went on and I gained his trust, Cory also confided to me the reason for his academic failures: he couldn't read. This was a source of embarrassment to him, a secret from his parents, and the reason he did poorly in school. He and I took on the challenge, embarking on a program to help him pass his GED. Ultimately, he didn't pass the test. But, in the end, he went on to achieve great success—and he taught me a vital lesson: to question my assumptions about intelligence.

Here's what happened. Discouraged and angry, in his junior year, Cory quit high school and enrolled in a race car mechanics course at a nationally known speedway. It was a big leap—at 17, he became the youngest member of a contingent of aspiring mechanics whose average age was 30. But Cory finished first in his class. Along the way, he appeared regularly on ESPN with several of the winning drivers of his cars. On completing the 18-week course, he received an offer to join a pit crew at the Indianapolis 500 Motor Speedway—the ultimate accolade.

Cory returned to visit me every so often after that, grateful for the GED help, even calling me the best teacher he'd ever had. Of course, mainly I had listened respectfully and allowed him to share his well-kept secret. His visits gave me the opportunity to probe the reasons for his success and his ability to perform as a really terrific mechanic. For starters, I wanted to know how he managed his way through all the engine manuals since he couldn't read. He didn't read them, he told me. Instead, he said, "In my mind, I can see how the engine comes apart and goes back together. It's like I have a picture to work from—it's easy."

Most educators have similar stories to tell. There are countless tales of kids who don't fit the mold of school, who demonstrate unusual talents, and who often succeed in spite of expectations. But Cory stuck with me. What Cory found easy would leave most valedictorians at a loss. That led me to ask, long after I had left teaching: Who is smarter? Who is more intelligent? What defines a person as intelligent?

In those days, one answer was clear: Cory wasn't smart *enough*. Academic mastery trumped all. But most teachers today notice a pronounced, but indefinable, shift in intelligence. The world operates by a new set of rules; so do the kids. How do we define these new skills and behaviors? How do we honor them? How do we assess them? How do we catch up to the new world?

Let's take the first step: let go of old beliefs about intelligence.

MOVING WITH THE TIMES

If, as a 12-year-old in 1900, you squeezed into an old wooden desk to take an IQ test, you would likely have encountered this question: What is the relationship between a dog and a rabbit?

Scanning the multiple-choice possibilities, the answer would have jumped out at you: *Dogs chase rabbits.*

Yes, dogs do indeed chase rabbits. Score one for higher intelligence.

But times change. Over a hundred years later, given the same question, a sharp 12-year-old would spot a quite different, but now more acceptable, answer: *Dogs and rabbits are both mammals.*

Which answer is correct? It depends, doesn't it? In some cultures, the answer might be, *Both dogs and rabbits are good to eat.* Or, maybe scribbled as a note beside the question, *I live in the city. What's a rabbit?*

Such results pinpoint an immediate problem with intelligence: the 12-year-old in 1900 was not unintelligent or less smart than a similar child a century later. On a modern IQ test, the average IQ of a person in that year would be scored at 67, consigning half of the world's pre–World War One population to the category of intellectually disabled or mentally retarded, if measured by today's standards.

But that can't be true. The world changed, not people. Or, to be more precise, the world and people changed together. One animal still chases another across a garden patch, but rural knowledge has less utility in the modern age. We've adapted to the times. Before we observed a plain old animal; now we see a mammal, and grouping dogs and rabbits in a class of vertebrates signifies your intelligence.

Modernizing the questions for IQ tests has yielded good results, however. IQ scores are rising three points every decade and, in some cases, nearly 20 points in a generation—gains so steep and sudden that scientists can't explain them. The most sensible explanation is that schools have done their job. James Flynn, author of books about IQ such as *What Is Intelligence?* (2009) and *Are We Getting Smarter?* (2012), attributes the rise to a scientific revolution that improves our ability to classify the world around us, based on increasing use of scientific logic. Known as the Flynn Effect, this theory posits that our use of "scientific spectacles" enables us to reflexively organize information into abstract categories and discern complex relationships between concepts.

As any student knows, these abilities conform to the exact skills expected in school. Thus, for Flynn and others, education and intelligence are irretrievably intertwined. Another expert, Richard Nisbett, in *Intelligence and How to Get It* (2010), reiterates this view. "Without formal education," he states, "a person is simply not going to be very bright—whether we measure intelligence by IQ tests or any other metric."

This is another *very big* red flag, waving to warn you and your children about how confused the subject of intelligence remains. Classifying mammals, or mastering algebra, or naming the capitals of countries is something learned in school, not because your genes make you smart. This view also assumes that you live somewhere north of the equator. Under the definition of many experts, no indigenous person in the depths of the Amazon, unschooled in the university but literate in the ways of creatures and plants, can be considered smart—unless they find their way to a university and score well on a test designed by western psychologists in the early 1900s. In a diverse, multifaceted, globalized world stretching from the rainforests to the tundra to the barrios, that's like saying no one can claim to be smart unless they manage a billion dollar hedge fund from a skyscraper in Manhattan. The rest of us are out of luck.

THE FAILURE OF *g*

Essentially, IQ testing grew out of the fond hope that tests could measure a single psychological capacity and that intelligence could be identified as a unique faculty with a fixed address: the brain. Though IQ tests quantify performance on different kinds of problems, scores on the various problems do correlate, giving rise to the assumption that a common cognitive source exists that underlies the different tasks. But given the hidden nature of this source, science had no recourse but statistical analysis. That line of reasoning led British psychologist and statistician Charles Spearman, in 1904, to label the secret center of intelligence as *g*, a symbol for *general intelligence.*

The *g* factor doesn't exist in any real way—it's a statistical artifact that correlates with cognitive tasks and increasing task complexity. Because it's a numerical outcome that results from factor analysis and complex algebra—and doesn't speak to the richness of interactions and abilities that intelligence implies—it's heavily criticized. But it correlates moderately well with heredity, indicating that some aspect of intelligence is transmitted genetically, and gives scientists a needed peg to measure changes in intelligence over the life span (which it clearly does.)

G survives, but barely, and mainly because without *g*, intelligence testing becomes nearly meaningless. Criticisms include the fact that *g* is a statistic without any known biological foundation, or that *g* in fact represents another permutation of school achievement. In a typical criticism, philosopher Jesse Prinz, author of *Beyond Human Nature* (2012), notes that *g* correlates with the cognitive abilities measured by IQ tests, but so would fencing or macramé, if these were the leading subjects taught in school.

Despite the criticism that *g*—and its handmaiden, IQ—measures individual performance on a cognitive test rather than true intelligence, *g* is now a placeholder for the belief that intelligence is a genetic given and a manageable construct that lends itself to measurement. In fact, it's very convenient. The hope of finding one number to measure intelligence feeds the industrial culture's need to rank and order its citizens, giving rise to all manner of offshoots traced to IQ testing, including standardized tests for children, screening for immigrants, fitness for military duty, and categorizing the developmentally disabled.

Can IQ give students a leg up? In some ways, yes. IQ is associated with social status, income, academic achievement, success at work, and projected life span, as well as indicating a general ability to manage life successfully. If you solve one kind of problem on an intelligence test, it seems you can also solve other, similar problems—a good reason for math teachers to like high IQ students. Scores between 90 and 110 are normal; over 120 is considered superior. If you score in the upper 2% of the population (usually, a score around 140), you can join Mensa, the society for very smart people.

So IQ retains its grip on the public's imagination, though few people remember how the score is calculated. Your *intelligence quotient,* derived from a standardized test in which the mean score is set at 100 within your age group, equals your mental age divided by your chronological age times 100. If you're 50 years of age, but test out as having the intelligence of a 44-year-old, your IQ ends up at 88 (100 x 44/50 = 88). That's low by the way, but not to worry. Many critics of IQ have observed that Einstein would probably score equally low. Einstein himself considered this beneficial, shrugging it off by saying, "My intellectual development was retarded, as a result of which I began to wonder about space and time."

Expanding Our Views on Smart

Our views on intelligence influence our interactions with students, so moving away from the cognitive thesis—the belief that success today depends primarily on cognitive skills that can be measured by IQ tests—is necessary. The culture is saturated with IQ, and the concept retains a simple appeal. In the words of recent popular author Paul Tough, author of *How Children Succeed* (2012), "The world it describes is so neat, so reassuringly linear, such a clear case of inputs *here* leading to output *there.*"

Let me give you an evidenced-based reason: beyond agreeing that IQ measures a small slice of human behavior, scientists, especially psychologists, cannot agree on much of anything about intelligence. As Robert Sternberg, a leading researcher, and his fellow authors candidly note in *Models of Intelligence,* an in-depth review of intelligence published by the American Psychological Association, the field of intelligence research has fallen apart (Sternberg, Lautrey, & Lubart, 2003).

That means that the essential meaning of intelligence—what it is, where it comes from, and how it can be measured—finds no common ground among the neuroscientists, behavioral experts, geneticists, psychometric specialists (the test makers), artificial intelligence and information-processing experts, and advocates for emotional intelligence or multiple intelligences who spar for attention, funding, and journal space. A behavioral neuropsychologist critical of attempts to define and measure intelligence summed up the quandary by calling the concept of intelligence a "myth" (Schlinger, 2003). Intelligence, in his view, is simply a label for behaviors in the context in which they are observed.

BUT ISN'T INTELLIGENCE HARDWIRED?

Long after the motor vehicle proved superior to horses, people saddled up to go to town. In the same way, popular beliefs about IQ continue to limit our views of the abilities of children. Mostly, most adults still believe that IQ is fixed and passed exclusively through genes—a cultural norm now deeply embedded in their children. I have talked with many a 14-year-old who blamed low math scores on mom's (or dad's) lack of ability. "I didn't get the math gene," I'm told.

This assertion not only haunts education, but ignores the fact that heritability is measured though populations, not through individuals, and that a one-to-one correlation in a genetic trait like eye color is quite different from math ability, which must rely on a large number of genes acting in concert to produce even the minimal capability to grab a pencil, take out a piece of paper, and read a math problem. But such comments highlight a barrier to breaking through to a higher level of intelligence: a majority of people continue to believe that intelligence is a predetermined, immutable, genetic asset or liability.

If you count yourself a believer, you can be excused. The misconception stems from the fact that, a short 20 years ago, intelligence was regarded as a fixed trait. Geneticists placed the heritability of IQ—the impact of the genes that hardwired your IQ scores—at 75–85%. In lay terms, that scientific conclusion translated into a grim fact: roughly, you had less than a 25% chance of improving your level of intelligence throughout your life. However enriching your environment, it would contribute little to improving your circumstances. Mental gymnastics, designed to bolster your intelligence, would likely fail.

Most reasonable investigators agree that small differences in IQ can be partially attributed to genes, but the "culture counts" argument has gained steady traction. Even as IQ and genetics grew popular in the 1920s, other psychologists advocated for *social intelligence* (Kihlstrom & Cantor, 2000). In this perspective, the main ingredients of intelligent behavior are developmental, including the ability of people to adapt, reflect, assess opportunities and risk, and engage their social environment in ways that are purposeful and strategic and lead to desired outcomes. Intelligence shifts as conditions change or one enters a new stage of the life cycle. As circumstances evolve, new regions of the brain, or even genes, may be activated.

Much of IQ testing supports now social intelligence theorists. When IQ is measured in less affluent or poverty-stricken households, it is found to be minimally important for success. Other factors—praise, love, care—count for more. Even brief messaging can change the equation. African American or Latino students enrolled in college, or females in math and science courses, score lower on tests when forewarned of stereotypes about achievements for their race or gender. The social psychologist Joshua Aronson, who investigated the impact of stereotypes and threat on performance, calls intelligence a "transaction among people" (e.g., see Nisbett, et al., 2012). That's a common view at present—and one I believe has far-reaching implications for teachers who want to foster more intelligent behavior in their students.

WHY *IS* INTELLIGENCE CHANGING?

There is more positive information from the scientific community about intelligence: humans appear to be getting smarter, at least as measured by IQ tests. Fluid intelligence, considered the ultimate cognitive ability underlying all mental skills, had been considered immutable, but in 2008, teams of researchers reported breakthrough results with studies indicating that fluid intelligence is "trainable." With 10 minutes of engaged practice on carefully designed computer games, children showed increased scores on measures of pattern recognition, an ability presumed to depend on perceptual speed, attention, and similar abilities (Jaeggi, Buschkuehl, Jonides, & Perrig, 2008).

The effects lasted six weeks, telling researchers that the brain requires constant fitness training (a common analogy), but the findings did set off another round of debate over the malleability of intelligence. Tapping into the fears of today's parents, the results also encouraged an entrepreneurial surge of brain-based computer games designed to improve test scores and chances for university admission.

Aside from the enhanced ability to categorize and use logic, children in recent decades demonstrate a clearly improved ability *to solve problems without being given a method.* On this section of the Wechsler Intelligence Score for Children, the chief IQ test used to identify children's cognitive strengths and weaknesses, scores have risen significantly. In other words, people, especially children, are getting better at figuring things out on their own. In a world with fewer guidelines and less moral clarity, this may be an adaptation.

In other ways as well, children's scores indicate that intelligence shifts with the times. During the advent of the digital revolution, verbal scores for adults shot up, but verbal scores for children remained static. The gap, identified originally in 1995 and surprising to researchers, is closing again. The theory? Children are now closer to their parents than in the 1960s and 1970s, with greater interaction leading to sharing of active vocabulary. And matching the folk wisdom, along with parental conversations, increased screen time and exposure to virtual technologies affects the brain as well: the spatial skills that children possess have risen significantly as well.

In another shift, women have begun to outscore men on IQ tests. One explanation is that women's increased access to higher education has improved scores. But again, no one can pinpoint the cause, nor do the recent overall gains in IQ scores since the 1990s—ranging from 9 to 20 points a generation—yield to an easy explanation. Even James Flynn's scientific categorization hypothesis doesn't satisfy most researchers, who cite better nutrition, the increasing complexity and cognitive requirements of modern life, smarter genes, or a technology-drenched life as other causes behind the shift.

YOU'RE AS SMART AS YOU BELIEVE YOU ARE

The most recent research has the most implications for teachers. Evidence confirms that beliefs and expectations held by teachers change intelligence. Carol Dweck, author of *Mindset* (2008) and a Stanford University professor and psychologist, used controlled experiments to demonstrate that when children are informed that intelligence is not fixed, their IQ increases. The secret, in Dweck's view, is that simple belief statements that support hope and optimism help children shift from a "fixed mindset" to a "growth mindset." Dweck identified what she regards as the key noncognitive factor behind the power of beliefs: purposeful engagement. In other words, if you desire to get smarter, or simply act as if you're smarter, you will be—at least, as measured by an IQ test.

No known neuronal connection links a belief to the brain, and some researchers believe that the cumulative actions of teachers treating children differently in a thousand small ways cause the change in IQ (MindShift, 2012). But the question remains: if each generation shows dramatic signs of getting smarter, what has triggered the adaptation? Either new genetic combinations have been activated by fast acting environmental inputs, or an unknown, rapid-fire mechanism has promoted a rich connective web of newly activated neurons. It is possible that the unexplained rise in IQ scores serves as one indicator of a shift. But the scores cannot be traced to genes; the rise is too dramatic and swift. Other factors, not yet understood, must be at work.

I'm certainly not the first critic of IQ, and I respect scientific efforts to figure out tough problems, so let's examine the roots of our muddle. First, defining and measuring intelligence suffers the same limitations that affect all deep inquiry into humans. Though researchers make valiant attempts to slice, dice, construct, theorize, and otherwise put intelligence into a convenient size package to be studied, it retains its black box status. In psychological terms, it's an *internal event*. It's not possible to peer far enough inside the body, brain, or mind to discern the origins of intelligence, nor can the exact parameters be drawn. It is still a mystery.

But let's take what the data give us. It's clear, at least for much of the world, whether by chance or due to the complexities of modern life, intelligence is on the move.

Moving Forward . . .

How Do You Feel About Intelligence?

1. *Examine your beliefs about intelligence.* So much of what happens in the classroom depends on your presence, including your hidden beliefs and biases (and we all have them). Intelligence can be a deeply personal subject, and most teachers have opinions on what makes students smart, or how they should be assessed, or their "potential" for learning.

   As you continue through the book, you'll have an opportunity to reflect on the following ideas. To get ready, do a quick check. How do you feel about the following statements?

   • Just as intelligence isn't narrowly focused or fixed, neither should education be anchored solely to traditional academic outcomes. To capture intelligent behavior, outcomes must be focused on a triad of performance indicators: (1) academic and content mastery; (2) skills for life, work, and citizenship; and (3) habits of mind or emotional competencies.

   • The changing definition of intelligence means that academic rigor needs to be defined in terms of individual skills and strengths, as well as content mastery, and not by the number of problems assigned for homework or the amount of reading crammed into an AP class. Cody's work as a mechanic qualified as "rigorous," but he failed traditional classes. That increasingly commonplace story describes children who are distractible, don't read well, and can't harness themselves to school—but who are highly creative, with great visual skills. It's likely that in the future, we will need to find ways to measure competency as a blend of creativity, problem solving, innovation, and self-reliance.

   • The fact that intelligent behavior also includes character virtues such as empathy, integrity, collaborative ability, and unbiased communication complicates the picture further. How do we activate these more subtle aspects of intelligence? And, again, how do we measure them?

   • In a chaotic global world, the idea that intelligence and environment are related takes on special significance. Will our world make children smarter or less so? And, more to the point, if intelligence is a function of beliefs about one's abilities, how do we convince every student he or she can be a genius?

2. *Test yourself.* Carol Dweck, author of *Mindset* (2008), offers a quick four-question online quiz to test your beliefs and assumptions about intelligence. See how you do! http://mindsetonline.com/testyourmindset/step1.php

Reflection Questions . . .

1. In what ways are you "smart"—or not?

2. Do you often use terms like *higher level* or *gifted* students? What do those terms mean to you?

3. Why do you think children are getting smarter, as measured by IQ tests?

3 Follow the Child
The "It" Factor

On a plane trip a few years back, I sat next to a hip young man, about 20 years old with an earring, an iPod, and a red ball cap on backwards, who was doing something that many young people don't. He was reading a serious book on politics and history. Ever on the lookout for success stories, I struck up a conversation about his education. Turns out, his account of how he educated himself caused me to wonder, again: How can schools help students become more intelligent for *their* world? Actually, after the conversation, the real question was a bit more negative: How can schools stop making young people *less* intelligent by continuing to impose too much seat time and a mid-century curriculum on them?

Here's the thumbnail: after spending two years at a community college, the young man had just won a full-ride Regents scholarship to the University of California at Irvine, a prestigious campus in southern California. Attending a two-year college out of high school had been his choice, he told me. Each of his three older siblings had graduated with 4.3 grade point averages from his highly regarded suburban high school—and he noticed that they all ended up hating high school. Too focused on grades, they felt stressed and time pressured. And, in an ironic twist, his sister was not accepted by the college of her choice because she hadn't participated in extracurricular activities. He also told me that earning a 4.3 GPA. wasn't a motivating challenge for him. "It's easy enough to get good grades in high school," he shrugged. "You just study all the time and don't do anything else."

His decision from ninth grade on? Focus on subjects that were meaningful to him; use the time saved for life-enhancing electives; become skillful rather than grub for grades. As a result, he turned his success in high school drama into a communications major at the community college, which he chose because of a strong connection to a supportive mentor there. Two years of stellar performance on the college debate team earned him the scholarship—a successful outcome by any measure.

I was even more impressed at the end of the conversation. How did my young friend plan to use his debate skills? Well, he thought he might go into real estate management. He knew how to manage money, he said, and now he wanted to manage someone else's.

WHAT'S "IT"?

His situation was different from Cory's, the young man in the last chapter. But it's another example of streets-smarts intelligence—the kind we wish we could teach in school.

Do we know how to do this? Not yet. Even if we take a traditional approach to intelligence, we can't make many factual assertions. Scientific speculation about changes in IQ scores is dampened by several omissions that become glaring in a multicultural, diverse global age. First, IQ testing is nearly always carried out among groups with access to education and nutrition, including college-age students, the go-to group for university researchers. No comparable data exists for nonindustrialized countries. So is everyone getting smarter, or just the segment of the population with access to schools and media? We don't know. In a global world beset by novel problems, and looking to extract gains in human performance, knowing whether everyone's intelligence is rising remains a mystery.

But we can say, without fear of contradiction, that around the world, people want to *get smart in a different way.* For example, if you search the online employment ads or the Sunday classifieds for a job, you discover it's true: categorizing rabbits and dogs ranks low on the list of desirable traits that employers seek. Nearly every job requires qualifications like the following, drawn from my local newspaper recently:

For a lower-level position in management:

- *The ability to explain complex information clearly*
- *Good communication and listening skills*
- *Excellent customer service skills*
- *Honest and trustworthy attitude*
- *An interest in legal and financial matters*
- *Good mathematical and computer skills*
- *Respect for confidential information*

I live on the west coast of the United States, so I cast a wider net and checked online ads in India. A customer service position advertised in *The Hindu,* an Indian business journal, required these skills:

- *Ability to communicate in any situation*
- *Strong customer service skills*
- *Attention to detail*
- *Organizational ability*
- *Computer literate*
- *Outgoing and fun personality*

Given global unemployment rates, you would assume no shortage of qualified applicants (or "fun" people) for these jobs. Not so. In fact, not nearly enough people seeking jobs can meet these requirements. In the same Indian journal, CEOs of banking and financial services said their new hires lacked skills in listening, team work, collaboration, and attitudes such as self-motivation, self-discipline, commitment, and dedication.

Around the world, this complaint is common from industry, as is the short-term solution: seek out young people who are trainable in these skills. As one Indian CEO put it, "We hire people for attitude and train them for the skills."

Attitude Equals Altitude

Attitude is the right term. In the global age, information flows at the touch of a button or voice command. What to do with the information, and how to apply it, is the modern challenge. That makes skillful behavior much more personal—and more difficult to teach. Persistence and autonomy please employers, but a manager can't graft those qualities onto an employee. That's the "it" factor, but companies don't even know the right questions to find out if employees have the "it."

If you want a glimpse of the problem, read the questions posed by interviewers these days to prospective employees (e.g., visit www.glassdoor.com). Off-topic interview questions are now the rage, such as, What's your favorite website? What makes you uncomfortable? Where do you vacation in the summer? Rather than probing for skills, these questions that have been compared to dating sites or choices of romantic partners (Hill, 2013).

Google has become particularly Internet-famous for screening prospective employees by posing puzzles or asking intentionally open-ended questions with no single correct answer. The interviewer's goal is to see how the thinking process of the applicant works, and to gauge his or her creativity in problem solving. Sample questions: How much toilet paper would you need to cover Texas? How many vacuum cleaners are made a year? Can you swim faster in water or in syrup? How would you weigh your head (Fottrell, 2014)?

The bad news is that the infamous puzzles or questions used at Google show no reliability as a guide to job performance; they've become a game to pressure applicants. In other words, companies are not certain how to measure or stimulate creativity, deep thinking, and the "it" factor, as I will call it in Chapter 4.

The other bad news is the same problem will overtake education. Beyond the industrial model lies a personalized, inquiry-based system focused on the skills of application, problem solving, and innovation. Success depends on activating, teaching, and assessing those aspects of human performance untouched by traditional testing and instruction. That's an issue, as authors Andrew Rotherham and Daniel Willingham (2009) tell us:

> Another curricular challenge is that we don't know how to teach self-direction, collaboration, and creativity the way we know how to teach long division. The plan of 21st century skills proponents seems to be to give students more experiences that will presumably develop these skills—for example, having them work in groups. But experience is not the same thing as practice. Experience means only that you use a skill; practice means that you try to improve by noticing what you are doing wrong and formulating strategies to do better. Practice also requires feedback, usually from someone more skillful than you are.

CLOSING THE GAP BETWEEN SCHOOL AND LIFE

You, as a teacher, are not alone in this struggle to redefine how to prepare students for life in the 21st century. Preeminent organizations such as Google know a secret that educators hesitate to share with parents: certification that denotes information mastery no longer counts as the main requirement for success. Google's senior vice president of people operations puts it bluntly: "G.P.A.'s are worthless criteria as a criteria for hiring, and test scores are worthless . . . we found that they don't predict anything" (Friedman, 2014).

Instead, Google has identified attributes of potential employees that forecast success much better than traditional notions of expertise. The first is a general "learning ability" unrelated to IQ, including the ability to process "on the fly" and "pull together disparate bits of information." A second is emergent leadership, the willingness and confidence to step in and step up at precisely the right moment. A third? Humility and ownership. This is the ability to be wrong and embrace a better idea, especially in collaborative teams. In other words, collaborate, adapt, and relearn.

That's the core issue for education: the skills listed in the ads are today's *life skills,* the kind of intelligent behaviors required to flourish in the dynamic, ever-shifting state of today's frenetic and somewhat unhinged global environment. These are *not* just work skills. The skills may qualify employees for the fast-paced, collaborative demands of the work world. But they also reflect the underlying attitudes necessary to engage the world, learn from experience, and view it through a thoughtful, intelligent lens.

In fact, they offer a perfect profile of today's lifelong learner. They arm a young person with the creative, flexible capacity to invent new technologies, design responsive global institutions, resolve geopolitical conflict, rebuild communities, or engage in innovation. But this statement alone explains the shortage of enough work-ready young people. Schools don't teach attitude—at least, not in a positive or intentional way. Nor have they evolved to the point that they teach essential global age skills. As Sir Ken Robinson, the creativity expert and critic of industrial education, suggests, schools "marginalize" the very skills necessary in today's work environment. He makes the point strongly: "In the work world, collaboration and team work are essential to success; in school, it's called cheating."

As the new standards begin to highlight collaboration and communication, this older view will shift. But hoping that schools will fill the skills gap through conventional instruction is misplaced. In days past, a manual could show a machine operator how to turn the crank to keep an assembly line rolling. Accountants could be shown how to line up the numbers down the page. And an experienced trainer can still teach a young person to dip uncooked potatoes into a vat of hot oil and produce French fries, or follow a script to troubleshoot a software issue, or perform rote tasks on an assembly line.

But now, teach someone to make eye contact with customers, communicate with sincerity, listen attentively, and respond to customer complaints or the sixth change on the same order without judgment or anger. Issue a directive to be self-motivated or have a "fun" personality. These skills don't conform to the old industrial definition. In fact, they're not skills at all; they're behaviors driven by personality and character, which meld into a kind of "it" factor that resists easy classification. At this point, "it" describes a subtle, people-sensitive, self-managing, internally balanced, purpose-driven individual with a positive sense of self who radiates a positive attitude, entrepreneurial energy, and a sense of competency.

THE NEW GLOBAL STANDARD

Roughly, the "it" factor portrays someone who is resilient, empathetic, flexible, curious, and persistent. In fact, it's likely you have seen this list before. Often, this list or something very similar is posted on bulletin boards in classrooms or hallways, or handed out as small laminated cards to students. Sometimes these qualities become "themes" of the month. The lists have also grown long, often including the attributes associated with sainthood or millionaires: ethical behavior, resourcefulness, self-awareness, hope and optimism, vision, initiative and entrepreneurialism, imagination, creativity, and etiquette in a diverse workplace.

It's quite likely this list will morph even further as the skills and competencies of 21st century life become better defined. In an article titled "What Machines Can't Do," *New York Times* columnist David Brooks (2014) writes about the effects of technology on his own field of journalism, which now rewards *sprinters* (people who can recognize and alertly post a message about some interesting immediate event) and *marathoners* (people who can write large conceptual stories), but which has hurt *middle-distance runners* (people who write 800-word summaries of yesterday's news conference).

Brooks speculates further that having a great memory and straight As is less important in a world that rewards enthusiasm (which stimulates curiosity), extended timelines and strategic discipline, procedural architects who can devise systems, the ability to manage loose teams and decentralized networks, and essentialists who grasp the core essence of a thing or topic. "The role of the human," he says, "is not to be dispassionate, depersonalized or neutral. It is precisely the emotive traits that are rewarded: the voracious lust for understanding, the enthusiasm for work, the ability to grasp the gist, the empathetic sensitivity to what will attract attention or linger in the mind."

No one can quarrel with these commendable lists. Teachers know about them and agree. But the issue remains: these *noncognitive outcomes* (an outmoded term, by the way) have not attained status in the system yet. Neither taught nor tested, they do not have equality with the core curriculum.

The problem shows up in two ways. First, the qualities posted on the wall have turned into hard assets crucial to success in both work and life. It's important to note here that work requirements (aside from technical expertise) and life skills are now one and the same. Teaching and assessing the "it" factor—the meld of strengths and skills—is now a necessity if adults want to make good on a promise to prepare students for *their* world.

A second, far more difficult, issue is that the "received" model of learning leaves teachers completely unprepared to deal with the inner life of children. Yet the new world requires that inner life be addressed and nurtured. "Thrive and drive" are real necessities, but they don't come out of a standardized curriculum. No wonder that students complain about feeling unchallenged. They float in a techno-sea of information, comply with lengthy requirements to retain standardized information, and endure formal instruction to meet life goals. But the cognitive, academic model fails to reach deeply inside to inspire them.

Variations meant to address the issue are increasingly numerous. Conversations about 21st century skills, inquiry, hybrid models, flipped classrooms, more technology, and a thousand other suggestions fly around in the form of policy papers, initiatives, blogs, or curriculum mandates. But rearranging deck chairs will not alter the course of the ship. Instead, let's think about reimagining schooling to reflect the inner life of a child and free the heart and brain to bring forth the exact skills necessary to be smart in today's world.

Instead of measuring difficulty in terms of information retrieval, or amount of homework, the new standard of *personal rigor* puts thinking and intelligent behaviors at the forefront. How a student expresses those personal qualities become the standard for capability and performance. In effect, we're starting to redefine what is "hard" in school.

Students like this new form of challenge. A 12th grader in my class, a girl with a 4.3 GPA. and impeccable bookwork skills, once remarked on the amount of collaboration and presentation skills she needed to master to succeed in our project-based environment. She was slightly puzzled, and frowned. "This class isn't *hard,*" she said, "it's just really challenging."

Assigning massive amounts of homework each night doesn't make school hard in a meaningful way; it's more a test of willpower. Willpower and perseverance have their place, but a system that values quantity of work over quality of thinking runs the risk of cynicism and disengagement—exactly the current situation with too many of those 4.3 GPA students. They do the work, but not with the passion that drives deeper learning.

FROM INTELLIGENCE TO INTELLIGENT BEHAVIORS

The young man I talked with in the airplane proved the point about IQ. He spoke with poise and authority, and it was clear that his success and range of skills had given him a kind of confidence to try something entirely new. That agrees with a more dynamic definition of intelligence that incorporates native ability, environmental influences, and personality into a holistic understanding of how people behave intelligently.

Should educators be doing the same? I think so. As noted psychologist Robert Sternberg and colleagues (2003) say, "In a world so beset with problems, perhaps the most important thing to understand is not the intelligence of people, but how they use it." But if we truly want to encourage intelligent behavior in schools—to prepare students for a world that demands that they make informed choices, manage uncertainty, and live by entrepreneurial norms—then we need to do more than simply abandon the outdated, "cognitive capsule" view of intelligence that spawned the current educational focus on fixed capacity and retention of information, as measured through high-stakes testing.

In fact, if we're going to help students be "smarter" by acting more intelligently, we're going to reexamine beliefs that have guided teachers since the days of the Model T. As you move through the next few chapters, consider your views on the following:

- *Intelligent behavior is not amenable to reward and punishment. Rather, students now ask, Is this worth doing?* Intelligent behavior draws students naturally to authentic tasks that contain meaning. That means educators must find a new balance between constructivism and accountability—between creative tasks and information. Bottom line: students need to be freed from the constraints of a rigid, fact-filled day, and offered flexible opportunities to pursue learning.

- *Intelligent behavior is mediated by personality; it is not an innate reflex. Mood, outlook, experience, goals, and communication style all impact behavior.* The trend toward personalized and differentiated instruction reflects what teachers know: A one-size-fits-all approach to learning does not really work. And the more we personalize, the more difficult it becomes to standardize. This conflict lies at the heart of discussions about the future of education. How do we create multiple pathways for inquiry and innovation—which are necessary to appeal to the broad range of talents and interests in today's youth—while still teaching a core curriculum?

- *Intelligent behavior is highly related to self-efficacy. Students will ask, Can I succeed at this?* As Chapter 5 will make clear, rigor should no longer be defined by the "hardness" of work, but instead should represent a standard for students' practical, adaptive skills, and their habits of mind. But personal mastery does not occur through lectures and testing—it happens through practice and feedback, with the teacher as a supportive mentor. In essence, if educators want to have students learn intelligent behaviors, they must become facilitators of learning— a big change from grading essays.

- *Intelligent behavior is a whole-body exercise.* The research cited in Chapter 2 tells us that motivation, perception, effort, and engagement— all central to intelligent behavior—do not arise solely in the brain. As data correlating school climate and academic achievement show, emotions and the environment impact cognition in powerful ways, both negatively and positively. For starters, that means letting go of the outdated distinction between cognitive and affective learning.

You might be reading the above and thinking, "Of course!" If so, consider yourself in the majority. Very few teachers doubt that a broad and diverse set of abilities serves students well, or that stressful emotions interfere with the clarity of their thoughts. It is a kind of commonsense version of intelligence.

But the disconnect between the deepest beliefs of teachers and the requirements of industrial teaching *is* surprising. Despite the relentless focus on academic achievement and test scores, most teachers see intelligent behaviors as more important than academic prowess.

Over a period of several years, I routinely asked teachers at the beginning of workshops to identify the core skills they wished for their students. But eventually I stopped. In every instance, rather than cite intellectual capacity, math competency, or knowledge of history, teachers pointed to communication, collaboration, empathy, and resiliency skills as their highest priorities.

How to explain this gap? Mostly, it can be traced to embedded assumptions about intelligence that have driven the *design* of our educational system. Think of the widespread notion that gifts are hardwired. On a recent trip to a state in the southwest United States, I learned that schools there use standardized measures to identify "gifted" children at the age of five, setting in motion 12 years of special attention, while other students remain categorized as "low" or "middle" achievers by the school system. That's a squandering of human capital that the world can ill afford.

Or consider the distinction between hard skills and soft skills. The former invokes the tensile requirements of an industrial economy; the latter implies a secondary set of skills that might make you a nicer person, but don't really count. Except now they do, and everyone knows it.

READY FOR A NEW MENTAL MODEL?

"How much easier it is to be critical than to be correct," said Disraeli, the controversial British Prime Minister and master politician, as he navigated the crosswinds of British industrial life at end of the 19th century.

Boy, is that true now. Everyone's a critic of a system of education produced by the industrial age. John Abbott (2010), director of the 21st Century Learning Initiative, says that "civilization is on the cusp of a metamorphosis," but schools continue their emphasis on feeding children static information and rewarding them for doing only what they're told, instead of helping them develop the transferable, higher order skills they need to become lifelong learners and thrive in an uncertain future. Daniel Pink (2009), author of the bestselling *Drive,* a book on motivation, calls education a "comply or defy" system that relies on outdated carrot and stick approach to learning. Stephen

Covey (2010), the world-renowned leadership expert, said just before his death, "The world has moved into one of the most profound eras of change in human history. Yet our children, for the most part, are simply not prepared for the new reality. The gap is widening. And we know it."

No one is completely wrong, and everyone has ideas. Abbott calls for replacing the machine-age metaphor that children are machine-like entities with the notion that they naturally observe, deconstruct, piece together, and create their own knowledge. Pink pushes for valuing effort over talent and inviting students to share their creativity and insight. Covey recommended focusing on the character strengths and competencies required to really succeed in the 21st century.

The list could go on and fill the book. Let's just say a consensus is evident: it's past time to let go of a narrow form of intelligence that makes our children less smart, in the sense that they become less capable of solving problems and using what they know, and find ways to integrate a new and broader view of intelligence into our daily work. The future view should reflect growth rather than deficits, combine skills with attitude, and honor intellect and knowledge.

This sounds simple enough, until we're brave enough to dig into unexamined assumptions that guide our work in the classroom. What we choose to believe about the intelligence of children closely tracks our assumptions about human nature (rationality is good, but emotions are bad), assumptions about the nature of knowledge and the way it is acquired (it's transmitted, not inherent), and assumptions about human potential (it's limited and fixed). These assumptions spawned an institutional mindset that still prevails (children won't learn unless you make them; children can't be trusted to learn on their own; children can't make intelligent decisions related to their education; all children learn the same way and have a similar rate of learning; see Clark, 1997).

Do we all believe these assumptions? No. In fact, most teachers would resist them. But it is indisputable that a set of industrial beliefs are ingrained in the mental model we call education. The assumptions may feel questionable now, but what replaces them? What new beliefs should we hold about students? What new mental model do we use to frame intelligent behaviors into a framework for teaching and learning? And to what extent will we risk changes to our beliefs? It's not easy to let go and experiment.

These questions challenge us, but that is the nature of times. As the Middle Ages gave way to the Renaissance that would result in the Enlightenment, Machiavelli had an explanation for the confusion in his world. "The times are too big for our brains," he said. It's not an excuse, but given that the 21st century seems a bigger show than the Enlightenment, it's a good reminder that these things take time to work out.

TOWARD A PERSONALIZED SYSTEM

I know these questions have been hanging around for quite some time now. The dichotomy between nurturing the inner life of children, which presumably speaks to and liberates their inner strengths, and harnessing them to a strict curriculum and set of standards that (hopefully) prepare them for postsecondary life, is well known to teachers. In many ways, it is *the* dilemma facing a thoughtful, caring teacher.

But in a world increasingly dependent on skilled application and less reliant on scarce information, the split seems particularly pernicious. In the words of Yong Zhao (2012b), the widely regarded advocate of global education and author of *World Class Learners,* it is time to "follow the child." That means, in Zhao's words,

> To prepare global, creative, and entrepreneurial talents, that is, everyone in the future, education should at first not harm any child who aspires to do so or suppress their curiosity, imagination, or desire to be different by imposing upon him or her contents and skills to be judged to be good for him or her by an external agency and thus depriving of the opportunity to explore and express on their own.

Student-centered is an increasingly popular term, so *following the child* is on our radar. It's become apparent to educators that the resources of the whole child must be harnessed to evoke the intelligent behaviors and personal strengths necessary for modern life. There is also widespread recognition of the consequences of the global information age, which includes an unsettling breakdown of the accepted canon for knowledge and an on-demand environment that makes standards feel obsolete as soon as written. All this mandates a shift to the individual and his or her talents.

But student-centered instruction at the moment serves as a cover for our inability to clearly articulate a coherent vision of our intended outcomes for students. When instruction flows from a body of pre-ordained information, it is impossible to design a true student-centered system. The legacy of the industrial system is that there must be rules for what children should know, and without those rules, Monday morning feels uncertain. If we don't impose our will on the child, what will they learn? What will they know? If we don't standardize the instruction and the assessment, how will we sort and select, reward performance, or ascertain the impact of our teaching and curriculum?

Mostly, thinking about the future and designing a new form of education that systematically focuses on the strengths, character, and attitude of students, rather than rewarding the accumulation of information, stops here. At that exact point, the times really do become "too big for our brains." Moving from the quantifiable apparatus of schooling to the qualitative expressions of deeper intelligence—and to more personal, individual standards for thinking and accomplishment—is a huge thought barrier to cross. Welcome to 21st century life.

Moving Forward . . .

Changing Your Mental Model of Education

Changing ideas about anything can be hard; it's even more difficult when a model like education has 1,500 years of history! But many minds are at work, sharing great ideas and insights. So two suggestions:

1. *Review your vocabulary.* Language reflects our metaphors, which emanate from mental models and belief systems. Think of the old "It went in one ear and out the other" or "at-risk" (who isn't?) or hundreds of other phrases that reflect deficits, negative emotions, and limitations. See if you can eliminate these from your conversations with students (and with yourself!).

2. *Explore the meaning of noncognitive skills.* So much of what will evolve in education will depend on a new national and global consensus around skills and attitudes. But the conversation often stops with old notions of cognition, as exemplified by the term *noncognitive skills*. Reflect on the term. Where do skills and attitudes come from?

Reflection Questions . . .

1. What steps can you take in your classroom to promote intelligent behaviors?

2. How do you define "hard" in your school?

3. Do you believe that attitude can be taught?

4 Reconnect Heart and Brain

Why Love Matters

Good teachers share one trait: they are truly present in the class room, deeply engaged with their students and their subject. . . . [They] are able to weave a complex web of connections among themselves, their subjects, and their students, so that their students can learn to weave a world for themselves. The connections made by good teachers are held not in their methods but in their hearts. (Palmer, 1998)

Quotes like the one above were once popular in education. But they've fallen out of favor, deemed too fuzzy by policy makers and educators focused on accountability. Measurement has replaced inspiration. This more recent approach to learning supposes that input, typically in the form of direct instruction of core content, can be linked to exact outcomes on high-stakes tests. At its best, it offers a narrow, but accurate, window into performance. At its worst, it encourages a laundry list approach to teaching, relying on pacing guides, whiteboards with daily objectives, and textbooks jam-packed with tips, strategies, and colorful graphics. In extreme form, it mandates that teachers educate kindergarteners by reading academically charged scripts to them, as proposed by some states in the United States (Korbey, 2014).

Few teachers argue against well-thought-out curricula, textbooks, standards, strict accountability, or even testing itself. But I have found that, while nearly all teachers respect advances that have helped the profession, their intuition tells them that something is missing. As I wrote earlier, this became clear when I asked teachers at workshops to name the outcomes they deemed most important to prepare students for 21st century life. Without exception, every group listed perseverance, resiliency, grit, curiosity, creativity, and empathy as top priorities. I was surprised to discover that I had to draw their attention back to academic achievement. When I did, they laughed and shrugged (and these were very good teachers!).

Why the dissonance? Because teachers sense that the present approach leaves us in a box. First, it's too reminiscent of the *old* world, from the days of industry and factories and a linear, orderly, Newtonian model of straightforward cause and effect, when in fact the world opening in front of us revolves around probabilities rather than certainties, intrinsic motivation rather than extrinsic controls, interconnectivity leading to multiple outcomes, and almost unlimited freedom for individuals to pursue what is significant to them. (See the work of Sam Chaltain, e.g., Chaltain, 2010.)

Second, where is the *heart* in today's system? Education has become entirely *cognitively* based—as if everything important in life depends exclusively on brain function. The cognitive worldview easily accommodates standardization, logical outcomes, extrinsic compliance, behavioral rewards, and a straightforward relationship between input and output. Smart, as the natural outcome, means getting straight As and remembering tons of information.

But teachers simply don't believe this. Whether they use the term or not, most teachers are *whole child* educators, interested in helping young people become resilient, purposeful, and satisfied with life. Academics matter, but not to the point of ignoring the fundamentals of human happiness. And, though teachers would like to see the heart make its way back into the classroom, it seems to have no place in the present system.

But in an inquiry-based, relationship-driven system that values and expects deeper learning, the heart assumes a new and critical role. You can't get at the intangibles of motivation and perseverance, activate curiosity and divergent thinking, or tap the well of creativity without engaging the heart.

THE RETURN OF THE WHOLE CHILD

Peter Senge (2006), in *The Fifth Discipline,* advocates "going upstream in time and place to discover the source of problems." The first stop in finding the headwaters of our dilemma is the split between cognition and feeling. If we pay attention to the research on positive emotions, it's clear the split lives more in our minds than in reality. Thus, the first step in molding a set of intelligent behaviors into a whole is to disregard approaches that define learning as solely a cognitive act.

In our brain-centric, cognitively oriented society, this is the last—and most difficult—mindshift for an educator. But the latest science, as you will shortly read, confirms what our ancestors intuitively knew: The heart is intimately involved in a regulatory system that uses emotions to fuel, support, and guide brain functions. The brain, with its limbic capability, moderates our impulses and helps us gain a metacognitive view of our emotional lives.

I distinguish this from the term *brain-based learning,* which encourages the full use of the brain, but assumes that an organ, even as powerful as the brain, acts in isolation. It doesn't. To fully activate the brain, the heart must be soothed as well. Love, care, and positive relationships sooth us like nothing else. Whole child education is no longer a "nice thing to do"—it's a necessity if we want students to reach the highest levels of performance.

Integrating Emotions and Intellect

Reconnecting heart and brain opens the door to fresh thinking about intelligence by integrating emotions into a more coherent view of what makes us smart. This is not the case at present. Wedded to cognition, we're prone to dividing intelligence into distinct branches, and then pretend they are not part of the same tree. Think of *emotional intelligence,* or EQ (or EI, in research circles), which bypasses cognition in favor of emotional competencies. EQ identifies abilities outside the realm of analytic reasoning, such as self-control, zeal, persistence, or the ability to motivate oneself, and was originally defined by Daniel Goleman (1995) "as the capacity to reason with emotion in four areas: to perceive emotion, to integrate it in thought, to understand it and manage it."

Similarly, some schools adopted strategies to teach students to develop their "multiple intelligences," the set of (now) nine distinct, but interrelated intelligences originally posited over 30 years ago by Howard Gardner in *Frames of Mind.* Gardner's (1983) theory has been enormously influential, puzzling both academic experts, who remained wedded to the IQ model, and cognitive scientists, who cannot identify neuronal correlates in the brain to support the theory.

Each of these approaches has pushed us forward to better delineate and highlight emotional strengths. And in contrast to the very constricted measure of IQ, accepting EQ and its cousins feels easy. IQ meets resistance because it fails to enlighten us about our emotional capacity, while EQ reasserts the innate capacity to display our intelligence through use of internal assets. It encourages self-awareness, empathy, coping with adversity, collaboration, improved relationships, and managing impulses—all essential strengths.

But dividing emotions from intellect has had obvious consequences. It allowed academic subjects to preoccupy the agenda, while the emotional lives of students became secondary. Even today, most of the work on emotional intelligence is left to posters, assemblies, themes of the month, or special classes and curricula for social-emotional learning, as opposed to academic learning, to help students learn empathy, assertion, or other socially competent skills.

Underpinning this model is the idea that minds work through the brain, which worked well when the goal was compliance, consumption, regimentation, and retention of static information. But this foundational pillar has crumbled. Learning has turned into a process, not a fixed outcome. Knowing how students arrived at their destination is equally important as the final product of their thinking. Seeing evidence of their intrinsic commitment to a quality solution is vital. Documenting whether their curiosity was provoked or stilled is central.

And, most critically, we must find a way to *teach* these qualities. For that, we need a method to make students smarter in ways that matter for their world. The research into positive emotions provides one window into the process. It's possible, we know now, to affect the emotional lives of students through exercising our own positive attitude.

But I'd like to go deeper now. A smile and a wave, or a pleasant interaction, make the classroom a happier place. But your underlying attitude of unconditional acceptance, fueled by respect and appreciation for the uniqueness of every student (even those who drive you crazy), matters most and results in the greatest degree of positive, observable changes in body and brain. The bottom line? *Love makes the brain work better.* And this process begins in the heart. Most people might intuitively agree on that point. But now there's evidence for this. In fact, let's return to the topic *du jour*: evidence-based education.

THE POWER OF CARE

To understand the mechanism, I'll start by returning to the work of Barbara Fredrickson, described in the first chapter, whose most recent studies focus on cognition and the brain. Fredrickson and other researchers want to understand how positivity affects optimal functioning—the integration of body, brain, and mind into a holistic state of heightened awareness, lucid thought, and expansive creativity. Even more, by linking positive emotions and the brain's infrastructure, they're looking at the question of whether the grand emotions associated with the best in human beings shift cognitive states or even rewire the brain.

What has been learned so far? Fredrickson applies her *broaden* hypothesis to the brain by hypothesizing that positive emotions widen the array of thoughts in the mind. "It is possible," her coauthor and she state, "that the experiences of certain positive emotions, such as joy, prompt individuals to discard time-tested or automatic (everyday) behavioral scripts and to pursue novel, creative, and often unscripted paths of thought and action" (Kok & Fredrickson, 2010).

That's the conclusion of a careful scientist, backed up by data. People experiencing positive emotions show "notably unusual" patterns of thought, such as openness to information and preferences for a wider array of behavioral options. Kok and Fredrickson reason that these tendencies represent the downstream consequences of a more basic cognitive shift, "in which the boundaries of awareness stretch open a bit further during positive emotional experiences, enabling people to connect the dots between disparate ideas and thereby act creatively, flexibly, and with greater sensitivity to future timelines."

That's a fine definition of inquiry. But it's also a good, self-generating cycle for students (and teachers) to get caught in. The spiral is bidirectional. That is, positive emotions increase your coping and resiliency strengths, cognitive resources, and physical health. In turn, as you flourish, you feel more positive. In fact, Fredrickson most recently added an offshoot to her broaden and build theory: The upward spiral theory of lifestyle change, hypothesizing that positive emotions alter body systems and reinforce lifestyle change through sustained adherence to health and positivity. There's even good recent evidence that psychological well-being affects genetic expression, leading to permanent changes in the brain and body (Fredrickson et al., 2013).

Fredrickson hypothesizes that loving interactions characterized by mutual care and shared positive emotions bring about a "positivity resonance," triggering "biobehavioral synchrony" during moments made potent by close alignment and mutual care (Fredrickson, 2009). Many examples exist of this kind of interaction. A mother feeling strong affection for her infant moves into a rhythm with the child, cooing and smiling, stimulating the release of oxytocin, the "hormone of love." Brain coupling—resonance of brain wave patterns—occurs between speaker and listener during moments of intense or emotional exchange. But what is the primary mechanism? Here's the clue: Heart and brain are intimately linked.

THE HEART–BRAIN PARTNERSHIP

Based on research in cardiology, neurology, and psychology, a new science of the heart is emerging that takes us well beyond the old view of the heart as a sentimental valentine or a simple pump. In reality, the heart plays a complex role in influencing and directing our nervous system, hormonal response, and energetic mechanisms—all the systems central to our health, emotional balance, and cognition. For example consider four new facts about the heart:

- The heart contains up to 30,000 neurons similar to those found in the cranial brain, which process information and act as a "heart-brain."
- 80% of nerve traffic goes *upward* from the heart to the brain, giving the heart significant influence over the brain.
- The heart regulates the autonomic nervous system, giving it a primary—and surprising—role in managing stress and preparing us for optimum performance.
- Positive emotions activate this heart-influenced network, with widespread beneficial impacts on the entire system of brain and body, while negative emotions inhibit the system, leading to more stress, impeded cognition, and chronic health disorders (McCraty, Atkinson, Tomasino, & Bradley, 2005).

The connection between the nervous system and the brain has been known to science for many years. Simply stated, the automatic nervous system has two reciprocal branches, one that speeds up when we need to be active or respond quickly (called the *sympathetic* branch) and one that slows down when we need to relax, be in a peaceful state or go to sleep (called the *parasympathetic* branch). When the nervous system is properly balanced, the brain responds by moving its focus from the hind brain—the fight-or-flight center—forward to the frontal lobes—the center for attention, focus, critical thinking, and planning.

The Connecting Link

If you're not interested in the entire nervous system (or too much science), I suggest one nerve to know: the vagus. The vagus is the 10th cranial nerve, or the "wandering nerve" (*vagus* is Latin for "wandering"), and it is an accurate description of this nerve, which emerges at the back of the skull and meanders to the abdomen with a number of branching nerves coming into contact with the heart, lungs, voice box, stomach, and ears, among other body parts.

The vagus carries incoming information from distant parts of the body, providing information about what the body is doing; it also transmits outgoing information which governs a range of reflex responses and thus acts as a key indicator of the balance between parasympathetic activation (the relaxation response) and sympathetic activation (the "ready for action" response) in the body.

The right balance gives you more autonomic flexibility—the ability to quickly modify respiration, heart rate, and arousal. It's also highly myelinated, meaning it can carry a lot of traffic in a hurry and rapidly regulate cardiac output to foster engagement and disengagement with the environment.

But perhaps its most crucial function is to transmit emotions upward to the brain, including positive emotions and a feeling of love. The vagus connects extensively into a mass of neurons in the heart and then feeds directly into the hind brain and spreads its message, via hormones and branches, into the midbrain and forebrain. In fact, psychophysiological researchers often say that mammals are designed to express love through the vagus (Porges, 2012).

The vagal nerve is crucial to our understanding of the heart's ability to affect thinking. Emotions have emotional consequences—and positive emotions matter. Subjects with optimal vagal functioning (known as *vagal tone*) show superior performance on cognitive tests, better working memory, more ability to direct attention, less impulsivity, and fewer negative responses to environmental stressors. It can signal the opposite effects as well. Children who experience severe stress show lower vagal tone, indicating less resilience and greater vulnerability to emotional distress. In some case, patients diagnosed with post-traumatic stress disorder can show such extreme parasympathetic activity that they, in effect, mimic the "freeze" response of reptiles faced with dire threat (McCraty et al., 2005).

The last bit of good news is that the vagal nerve acts reciprocally. If it's working optimally, you feel better. Physiology and emotions reinforce one another. This, in essence, gives you a tool for modulating your emotions. For example, Fredrickson and colleagues investigated the impact of Loving Kindness Meditation (LKM), a mindful exercise that trains the mind to focus on positive thoughts. LKM predicted a greater experience of positive emotions, which were reflected in the vagal response (Salzberg, 1995). Similar investigations showed that positive emotions promote psychologically resilient individuals who also become more physiologically resilient as well (Tugade & Fredrickson, 2002). These studies go a long way to explaining why the current programs in mindfulness are having good results. There are ways to calm down the body and perk up the brain.

IS THE HEART "INTELLIGENT"?

There's always a physiological backstory to emotions. That is, when you feel something, it's because your body is experiencing a physiological effect. Emotions do not arise independent of the body. Rather, neurological and hormonal information flows from an array of bodily systems and organs to the brain, influencing centers in the midbrain involved in perception and emotional processing, which we then label an emotion.

The brain, in turn, provides the biochemical bridges that link key components of the mental and emotional systems into a whole. The cortex, for example, located at the front of the brain and responsible for executive functions, contains a host of receptors associated with emotional processing, indicating that cooperation between mental and emotional systems is essential for the expression of the full range of mental capacities, including attention, influence memory, and judgment (Damasio, 1994). It is possible, in fact, that the impact of emotions on clear thinking may be greater than we anticipated: the actual number of neural connections that bring emotional information *to* the cortex outnumber the pathways coming *from* the cortex.

What Does the Heart "Know"—and How Does It Tell Us?

The heart is able, as we now know, to signal the brain by using a code or language that the brain understands. One of the key breakthroughs in recent years has been to decipher this signal and understand how it is transmitted from the heart to the brain.

Contrary to popular belief, the heart does not beat with monotonous regularity, but varies from moment to moment. The term *heart rate variability* (HRV) is used to describe these naturally occurring, beat-to-beat changes in heart rate. HRV reflects the dynamic interplay between the nervous, hormonal, blood pressure, and energetic systems in the body, as these respective systems feed information back to the heart on the physiological and emotional state of the body. Most prominently, HRV reflects the balance between the parasympathetic and sympathetic nerves—a crucial indicator of whether the body is in a relaxed or active state.

Recent research has revealed that HRV is remarkably responsive to emotions. As the neurons in the heart process feelings or receive feedback from other systems in the body, the heart responds by varying its beat-to-beat intervals—a change that can be graphed in the form of a rhythmic pattern, or *heart rhythms*. Stressful emotions such as fear, anxiety, and anger result in an erratic and disordered heart rhythms.

In contrast, sustained positive emotions generate a smooth, ordered, sine-wave-like pattern. Through the use of recently developed technology, the rhythms can be displayed on a computer screen, giving us a window into the state of our emotions, as Figure 4.1 shows.

These two distinct patterns can be classified as *coherent* or *incoherent*— a key finding that enables us to match a student's emotional state to his or her performance in school. The coherent state is characterized by increased synchronization between the activity of the heart and brain, as the coherent rhythms travel upward from the heart, through the parasympathetic nerves,

Figure 4.1 Emotions are reflected in heart rhythm patterns.

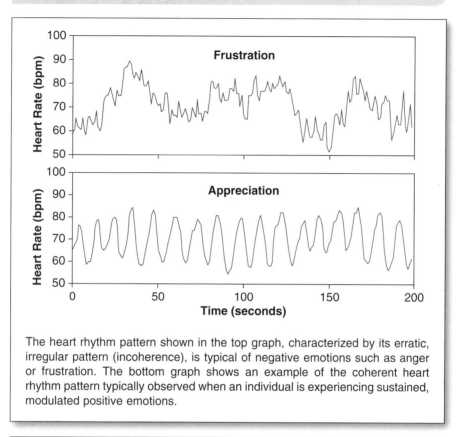

The heart rhythm pattern shown in the top graph, characterized by its erratic, irregular pattern (incoherence), is typical of negative emotions such as anger or frustration. The bottom graph shows an example of the coherent heart rhythm pattern typically observed when an individual is experiencing sustained, modulated positive emotions.

Source: Institute of Heartmath.

and into the hind brain, where the signals are distributed to the midbrain and cortex. The brain responds accordingly. With greater parasympathetic input, the brain's alpha and beta rhythms, as well as lower frequency brain activity, exhibit increased synchronization. Psychologically and physiologically, coherence is associated with a calm, emotionally balanced, yet alert and responsive state. According to Rollin McCraty, director of research for the Institute of HeartMath, it correlates with improved cognitive and task performance, including problem solving, decision making, long-term memory, and attentional focus (McCraty et al., 2005).

Incoherence, on the other hand, disrupts the brain and taxes the nervous system and bodily organs, especially if the heart rhythms remain chronically desynchronized by recurring or ongoing stress. The chaotic patterns impair cognitive functions and diminish one's ability to think clearly, make good behavioral decisions, and self-regulate emotions.

Taken together, these facts point to a kind of "heart intelligence"—a second center, along with the brain, which directs vital processes that underlie learning and performance. With every beat, the heart exerts its unique and far-reaching influence, sending out complex patterns of neurological, hormonal, pressure, and electromagnetic information. The heart's neural circuitry enables it to learn, remember, make decisions independent of the cranial brain, and even override the brain when necessary. In every way, the heart is a full partner with the brain in processing and applying information, as well as influencing a range of mental and physical activities.

These findings work against the prevailing deficit model of human strengths now widely accepted in education. The new heart also challenges many of our assumptions about learning. What we believe about intelligence—that it must come from the brain or is purely a cognitive function—may in fact be a barrier to accepting more heart-based approaches to education.

APPRECIATION: THE ULTIMATE TOOL

By itself, the heart is only as powerful as the intention and emotions that guide it. It's clear that positive emotions lead to greater physical and emotional well-being—and, in the case of students, to increased achievement, better performance, and improved behavior (Bradley, McCraty, Atkinson, Arguelles, & Rees, 2006). There are techniques, by the way, that students can use to generate positive emotions and shift their physiology, including patterns of brain activity.

But now for the key finding: *your* attitude can do the same for your students.

I consider the above statement to be the most important assertion in the entire book. Successful inquiry depends on a high-performing brain, but that may not be possible unless our attitudes match the requirements of love and acceptance necessary for the brain to function at exceptional levels.

First, another revelation about the heart. The heart is the most powerful generator of electromagnetic energy in the body, producing 5,000 times more such energy than the brain. As the heart beats, it produces an electromagnetic field about 50 times more powerful than the electrical energy generated by the brain. The heart's field can be detected anywhere on the surface of the body as well as up to six feet away from the body in all directions (the field of the brain, on the other hand, extends only a few inches from the body). This field is an important carrier of emotional information, and therefore mediates the energetic interactions between people (McCraty, 2002).

Most people think of social communication solely in terms of overt signals expressed through language, voice qualities, gestures, facial expressions, and body movements. But a subtle yet influential "energetic" communication system operates just below our conscious awareness, driven by the heart. These energetic interactions likely contribute to the "magnetic" attractions or repulsions that occur between individuals; they also affect social exchanges and relationships, communicating emotional and social information between individuals. In plain terms, the state of your heart is communicated to those around you.

Moreover, those feelings associated with appreciation, gratitude, and love, whether generated spontaneously or intentionally, evoke the heart's most definitive response—and thus have the most powerful influence over the brain. They produce the most harmonious heart rhythms, which, in turn, influence the brain and body so that students respond by becoming calm, emotionally balanced, highly alert, and more responsive (McCraty & Childre, 2004).

All teachers have walked into a classroom knowing immediately, without a word being spoken, whether the next hour was going to be challenging or invigorating. Now we know the reason: the signal emitted by the heart extends beyond the body, affecting the very atmosphere of a room and the quality of the day.

The electromagnetic exchange takes place when people touch. When two people touch, one person's heart signal (electrocardiogram) is registered in another's brain waves (electroencephalogram) and elsewhere on the other person's body (see Figure 4.2).

However, while this signal is strongest when people are in contact, it is still detectable when subjects are in close proximity. Researchers found that heart–brain synchronization can occur between two people separated by a distance of five feet when they interact, and that when people achieve a kind of physical and emotional connection they become more sensitive to the subtle signals communicated by those around them.

What can we learn from this research, and how do you take it forward in your classroom? That's the subject of the following six chapters, which focus on methods for relating to students, coaching and assessing them, and stimulating superior performance. As you move through the chapters, keep the heart in mind. The heart tells us that positive emotional states can be contagious, and that teachers who create positive, nurturing, energetic classrooms will likely enhance their students' motivation and receptivity to learning. And once students are more motivated to learn, they are more likely to carry that positive classroom influence to other classrooms and playgrounds, to their homes, and into their lives.

Figure 4.2 The Electricity of Touch: Heartbeat Signal Averaged Waveforms

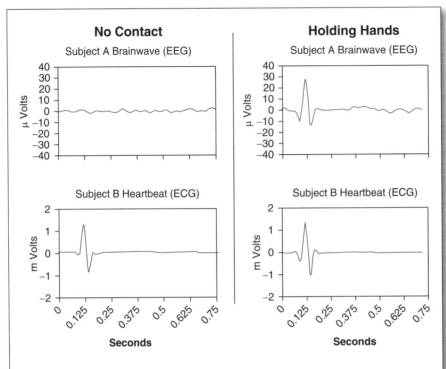

Signal averaged waveforms showing the registration of electromagnetic energy generated by one person's heart in another person's brain waves when they hold hands. The baseline recording (left column) is from a 10-minute period during which time the subjects were seated four feet apart without physical contact. The right column shows the recording from a five-minute period during which the subjects held hands. Note the appearance of Subject B's heart signal (ECG) in Subject A's brain waves (EEG) in the right-hand graphs.

Moving Forward . . .

Connecting With Students

1. ***Steps to connecting with students.*** So much of what you do as an inquiry-based teacher depends on your ability to connect with students, withhold judgment, remain open to novel solutions, let go of your role as the expert, and listen—*really listen*—to students. None of this comes easily to any of us, in the classroom or in other aspects of our lives. Mostly, you will benefit from feeling calm, centered, and open in an inquiry-based classroom. This is the province of *mindfulness,*

a state of active, open attention on the present in which you pay attention to thoughts and feelings without judging them. Research over the past few decades has found that mindfulness training develops *attention and concentration, social-emotional awareness, body awareness and coordination, and interpersonal skills. For more information, see the articles about mindfulness at greatergood.berkeley.edu.*

2. ***Take a new look at the heart.*** The old view of the heart as merely a pump has been completely revised through scientific advances over the last 20 years. For example, the heart is a hormonal organ, secreting oxytocin, the hormone of love (surprise). It also contains upwards of 30,000 neurons that act as a functional brain in the heart. It's also known that 80% of the nerve impulses between heart and brain travel *from* the heart *to* the brain, reminding us that the brain is not always in charge. In fact, it's more accurate to think in terms of a heart–brain partnership that directs the brain and body, and that acts as a receiving system for information coming from other parts of the body. For more on the new heart, go to www.heartmath.org.

3. ***Start simple: care, mastery, and meaning.*** The power of care has been well documented in the literature from the fields of youth development, adolescent mental health, risk and resiliency, and developmental psychology. All reports converge around one fact: a powerful, positive connection between an adult mentor and a young person greatly increases the likelihood of success in life. Reports available at chks .wested.org demonstrate the healthy outcomes from caring environments and positive school climate. For inquiry-based educators, this research has special meaning. Once a positive caring relationship is established between a mentor and a student, the teacher-mentor can have substantive, attentive conversations around a student's desire for meaningful and purposeful work, as well as open a "channel of trust" that allows students to receive feedback and work toward mastery.

Reflection Questions . . .

1. In your experience, have you witnessed how appreciation and care can change a student's performance and behavior?

2. It's easier to practice "whole child" education at the primary level. Can it also be practiced at the secondary level?

3. Do you believe it is possible to practice nonjudgment and unconditional support for every student?

Part II

Aligning School and Smart

5 Leverage the Power of Care

From Teacher to Mentor

From *hal,* the Anglo-Saxon word for health (and the root of *holy* and similar words), comes *wholeness,* a term that reminds us not just of the past but alerts us to a future in which education and healthy emotional development fit together in a seamless, coherent whole. In world that made perfect sense, this would be unquestioned, as it did to our prescientific ancestors who were not yet focused on the absolute value of cognition.

But I suggest we may come full circle. The surfacing of intelligent behaviors and deeper aspects of personality as keys to success in 21st century life tell us clearly that mind, body, and brain must work as a team—and that wholeness counts. It is our job as educators to close the gap and help young people activate every resource they possess.

A strange irony prevails here. Education values evidence-based findings. Yet, the most puzzling aspect of "evidence-based" education from the past decade is that it stands in direct opposition to 40 years of research from the fields of youth development, adolescent mental health, and developmental psychology confirming the conditions under which young people have the greatest chance of becoming successful adults.

This body of research falls together into the category of *resiliency,* but as experts have shown, resiliency is not just a means of coping with stress or trauma, but a universal capacity that mirrors the process of healthy human development (Benard, 1991). It's a broad term that encompasses social competence (such as communication, collaboration, and empathy), problem solving (such as planning, flexibility, and critical thinking), autonomy (such as initiative, self-control, and mastery), and a sense of purpose (such as motivation, creativity, and imagination) (Benard, 2004). In fact, think of resiliency as a short-hand notation for the blend of skills and strengths critical to navigating a challenging world.

A misunderstood, but vital, fact for educators to understand is that resiliency pertains to *all* youth, not just the "at-risk" category cataloged by the current educational system. If we look out on a 21st century landscape that contains far more chaos and uncertainty than previous eras—that, in fact, has stress built into daily life—the value of resiliency becomes paramount. It speaks to strengths, not deficits; it promotes wellness; it tells us that, with proper supports, nearly every child can become a self-directed, self-managing individual.

INTEGRATING HUMAN AND ACADEMIC DEVELOPMENT

Supporting and nurturing resilience in children is not a mystery. Research has converged around three core protective factors essential to supporting resilient behaviors (really, intelligent behaviors) in your students. Outside of education, these factors are gospel; inside of education, they stay well below the radar. But importantly, these factors have been incorporated into the fields of human performance, organizational psychology, positive psychology, and emotional intelligence—all the fields focused on improving achievement, success, and well-being. Why? They identify the conditions that maximize individual effort and the desire to achieve—the exact goals of a personalized, student-driven system of learning.

These factors can be condensed into three simple bullet points:

- *Caring relationships.* People perform better when they feel attended to. A caring relationship begins with recognizing and respecting the *autonomy* of the individual.
- *The desire for meaning.* Human beings work harder—on behalf of themselves or others—when they find purpose. The goal must be relevant to the person's needs and desires.
- *The power of mastery.* Achievement is a natural state of being. People enjoy doing tasks well and feel an intrinsic reward that perpetuates a spiral of further achievement.

It's easy to read this list and quickly move on. It sounds familiar to any teacher. But behind this simple list lie the fundamental principles for founding inquiry-based education in the 21st century. The overall goal is to design a system that integrates human and academic development by tapping into the deepest reserves of young people. These principles provide a way forward.

Increasingly, that's the direction of research into schools themselves. Another report on student performance was released a few days before this chapter was written. Conducted by Gallup Education, the "State of America's Schools" poll had good news: students who strongly agree that they have at least one teacher who makes them "feel excited about the future" and that their school is "committed to building the strengths of each student" are 30 times more likely than students who strongly disagree with those statements to show other signs of engagement in the classroom—a key predictor of academic success.

The report went on: "A broad focus on testing and new standards can lead schools to neglect the individualized social and emotional needs of students. These elements are often overlooked in the effort to "fix" America's education system, but there is growing recognition that unless U.S. schools can better align learning strategies and objectives with fundamental aspects of human nature, they will always struggle to help students achieve their full potential" (Blad, 2014).

Teachers recognize the central importance of engaging students through connection to the social and emotional side of students. For example, nearly half of teachers in a recent survey focused on the intangible connection between teacher and students as the key factor in engaging students ("Ed Pulse," 2014):

Social-emotional factors have so far remained optional. No longer. Inquiry requires a learner-centered ecosystem and "thrive and drive" environment that offers students the maximum opportunity for success. Focusing your teaching in this way doesn't require that you become an expert psychologist or mind reader. It's more a matter of new thinking and a fresh approach to the job in which you begin to operationalize the principles of human development.

INVERTING THE PARADIGM

Let's take a moment to define terms. What is *inquiry?* It's a multifaceted concept, held together by the core attitude of questioning and a core tenet: students take charge of their learning.

For nearly half a century, school reform has been centered on *inputs.* Writing better standards, improving discipline and class management, offering more compelling textbooks, integrating technology, or finding more money to do the same thing, only better, all represent fixes to the present system. The hope is that the fixes will finally keep students on task and engage them *deeply* in learning. Yet, after 30 years of continuous surveys of American high schools, students still report that their views on learning haven't changed (Wiggins, 2014a).

So what's the problem? Rather than improvement to the supply side, it's time to focus on the demand side. There is a momentous, broad-based cultural shift underway that has struck at the roots of every industrialized system of education. The result is a demand for more personalized learning, brain-friendly environments, less recall and more thoughtful application of knowledge, optimal conditions for eliciting intelligent behaviors, constructivist tools, and respectful, caring relationships that honor the learner above exalting the teacher.

Leading school-reform expert Michael Fullan puts it this way: "The worst thing a system can do is load up on standards and assessments in a way that overwhelms schools. This is the wrong driver number one. Instead, we have to focus on instruction and learning personalized to each student as the centerpiece, and then link to standards and assessments" (Rubin, 2011).

Voice and Choice

There's a simple way to describe the shift and its impact on teachers: The transformation in the world mandates more *voice and choice.*

That's what students want. We can balk, dally, defer, hide, or wrap ourselves in flags or tradition, but either we yield power to the new generation or they will take it. Think homeschooling, charters, hybrids, games, informal learning, online degrees, MOOCS, or a thousand other end runs around the traditional system. They'll find ways to learn according to the necessities of their time, not ours. Voice and choice bring forth the qualities of heart, mind, and skillfulness essential to 21st century life. That's the secret sauce. Only through a partnership with students—not a teacher-dominated, rigid, pacing guide kind of system—can education get where it wants to go.

Turning voice and choice into an everyday recipe will take time. Voice and choice is not a stand-alone classroom strategy; at its heart, it challenges the current education paradigm. For example, Students at the Center, a leading organization linked to Harvard University and research on the mind/brain sciences, learning theory, and youth development, cites four tenets of student-centered approaches that are essential to full engagement and deeper learning (www.studentsatthecenter.org):

1. *Learning is personalized.* Each student is known well by adults and peers in the learning environment and hence experiences learning as both a personal and collective good/process. Students benefit from individually paced learning tasks, tailored to start from where the student is and to address individual needs and interests.

2. *Learning is competency based.* Students move ahead based primarily on demonstrating key learning milestones along the path to mastery of core competencies and bodies of knowledge, rather than on a student's age or hours logged in the classroom. Tasks and learning units might be either individual or collective, and students have multiple means and opportunities to demonstrate mastery.

3. *Learning takes place anytime, anywhere.* Time is fully utilized to optimize and extend student learning and to allow for educators to engage in reflection and planning. Students have equitable opportunities to learn outside of the typical school day and year in a variety of settings, take advantage of the variety of digital technologies that can enhance learning, and receive credit for this learning based on demonstration of skills and knowledge. The school's walls are permeable—benefitting from multiple community assets and digital resources.

4. *Students exert ownership over their learning.* Students understand how to get "smarter" by applying effort strategically to learning tasks in the different domains. They have frequent opportunities to direct and to reflect and improve on their own learning progression through formative assessments that help them understand their own strengths and learning challenges. Students take increasing responsibility for their own learning, using strategies for self-regulation when necessary.

It's a good list, but it needs a fifth tenet: *Personalized learning is guided by an effective mentor and coach.* The industrial system of learning was quite good at its chief task: to transmit information or *in*-struct knowledge. But intelligent behaviors—the smart knowledge that must replace purely cognitive and academic outcomes—can only be nurtured. These behaviors can't be imposed; they must be elicited. So inevitably, there's an element of *con*-struct. But students need direction and guidance—an adult in the room, at their side. Helping students navigate between the poles of questioning and assembling a knowledge base requires a teacher-partner who understands the difference and the journey.

This is most often the missing link in discussions about the future of education, in my view. What is the exact role of the teacher, if not to instruct?

TOWARD "PERSONALIZED" TEACHING

I began the book on the note *Be the change you wish to see* for good reason. It is common to speak about the shift to personalized learning, but *personalized teaching* is more critical. Helping students grow the right attitude and demonstrate 21st century skills is fueled by a teacher's deep appreciation of what it takes for students to master skills instead of accumulating knowledge. Your personality and style, the willingness to establish positive relationships, a sincere regard for students, and openness to the failure and success cycle of discovery among them—all of these factors and more directly affect the quality of thinking and engagement, and thus the level of mastery in your classroom.

Most teachers care about students; that's not the issue. The greater challenge is to use that care and connection to drive deeper learning by thinking intentionally about how care interacts with purpose and mastery. In my workshops on project-based learning, I've often addressed this topic. When a teacher moves to an inquiry-based classroom, and in the process gets "off the stage," the dynamics of the teacher–student relationships shift also.

I call it moving from classroom management to "people" management. Classroom management depends on controlling student behavior with techniques backed by extrinsic rewards or sanctions. People management relies on the intrinsic motivation which surfaces when students feel engaged in an authentic, challenging endeavor. As every teacher knows, if students are happily learning, behavior issues virtually disappear in a classroom.

Becoming "Open"

The difference between classroom management and people management is no small matter. In the old world, teachers instruct, a one-way communication; in the new world, teachers partner, sometimes instructing, but also mentoring, co-learning, and facilitating expression. Underneath these roles lies a deeper subtext: mostly, you will need to be able to read your students and judge their internal progress. That requires a channel of trust between student and teacher. That isn't just a nice thing to do, but essential for helping students build the internal assets necessary for intelligent behaviors critical to 21st century performance.

I've often told audiences interested in project-based learning, my specialty, that a simple test of your Openness to Experience (Google it), one of five major traits identified in psychology as fundamental to human personalities, will give you a clue to your ability to perform this role. To be an inquiry-based teacher, you must be on good terms with the unknown, in more ways than one. For starters, you won't always know the outcome of an inquiry-based learning experience; it relies more on the process of learning than defined outcomes. Those teachers who succeed find they can dance above the fray a bit, see another's point of view, and engage collaboratively with students in the pursuit of trying to figure out best answers to open-ended problems.

Quite interestingly, the work world faces the same issue. Google again serves as an example. A recent article described the quality that made Google employees most effective as collaborative members of a team. The answer—*humility*—may surprise you. Those people who displayed that quality found it easiest to listen to and accept the ideas and viewpoints of colleagues, *despite* their own ideas and preferences (Friedman, 2014). So you, as an inquiry-based teacher, have the opportunity to model the same workforce skill.

Before ending this section, I want to emphasize that I understand that a focus on inquiry paints an optimistic and not altogether current picture of present schooling. We're still moving in fits and starts as the questions of standards, deeper thinking, and a more skill-based curriculum play out. That's the subject of the next chapter.

But the target is pretty clear: we're headed toward a kind of education in which skills, personal strengths, and the qualities associated self-guided inquiry are prominent features. New norms for creativity, collaboration, and critical thinking are in ascendance. Nearly everyone recognizes the essential value of teaching young people perseverance, resiliency, and empathy in a diverse, fast-paced global world. If the industrial paradigm still held, we wouldn't be shifting our emphasis in the classroom (though it might be a humane step). But the new world leaves us no choice. We either develop people to handle themselves or we're in trouble.

Our greatest barrier to accomplishing this goal may be another standard of openness: our ability to accept the world *as it is*. A world radically different from the past has come into existence, requiring more than mottos. To live happily in this new world, let alone master it, humans have to function at a fundamentally higher (and deeper) level than in previous eras.

CONNECTED COMMUNICATION: THE POWER OF THE MENTOR

It's also now possible to add to our discussion of the difference between the guide on the side and a more active mentoring role. The mentor relationship is now founded on the "teacher as brain changer" approach described earlier (Pillars, 2011). This approach takes into account the latest neuroscience of learning, which tells us that neurons are *active,* transmitting messages to one another and constantly altering a child's brain. The new model also encompasses research from social neuroscience showing that neurons in surrounding brains *mirror* one another. Activity in one brain quite often stimulates a similar area of a nearby brain. And research into the heart adds the final missing piece: positive emotions transmitted through the heart to the brain spread from the hind brain into the limbic system and frontal lobes.

The physiological changes alone dictate a 21st century version of mentorship: a connected communication model that emphasizes conversations with students rather than momentary interactions; nonjudgmental relationships that lead to openness; and simple, truthful, authentic exchanges that rely on sincere, attentive listening. Bob and Megan Tschannen-Moran, authors of *Evocative Coaching* (2010), wrote their book to describe how this model benefits the coaching of teachers, in which the goal of the instructional coach is to motivate and empower teachers rather than identify and fix weaknesses through the typical use of "constructive criticism." But it can also be adapted by teachers as a student-centered, no-fault, strengths-based coaching model that reframes difficulties and challenges as opportunities to grow and learn. At the core of the model is a kind of "dynamic dance" that relies on empathy and appreciative, strengths-oriented inquiry rather than an analytic, deficits-based conversation to improve performance and offer feedback that students can *hear*.

This reinforces the rationale for caring, connected communication. Fostering intelligent behaviors and deeper learning won't occur without an appreciative interest in the whole person or in the absence of caring relationships and empathetic interactions. Moving from finger-wagging to a growth-fostering psychology is now a necessity, not just a nice thing to do.

Building on the best that students can do, trusting in strengths, and disregarding the annoying behaviors that drive teachers to occasionally kick wastebaskets across the room (as I once did) is a challenge to any adult, let alone a teacher in charge of 150 lives during a day. So let's not be naïve here. You are not expected to be Gandhi or qualify for sainthood. In fact, it's not necessary.

The key is sincere appreciation for the possibility of human change and potential. You may lose your temper, but you never lose hope. Confronted by lack of progress or distant, unreachable students, you hold both skepticism and optimism as *one* thing. I will steal a term and call it *critical optimism*—the belief that capability for good or accomplishment, on some scale, lies within each of us (Mehta & Fine, 2014).

In the collaborative, less-hierarchical, dynamic world of today, becoming a *mentor* is a new mandate for teachers. Eliciting good attitudes from students requires having conversations with students about the meaning and fulfillment they seek in life (what are their interests?) and about their performance (I'm going to tell you how well you are doing and you trust me enough to listen).

This is the key to releasing the deep wellspring of ability—whether the will or skill—that results in deeper learning and the surfacing of resiliency, empathy, curiosity, perseverance, and flexibility. So simple, so difficult.

CRAFTING A "THRIVE AND DRIVE" ECOSYSTEM

Of course, it's possible to respond by asking, Don't we already care for students? Don't we hold out the best for them and believe in their success?

The answer is, Well, kind of.

Certainly the vast number of posters, exhortations, mottos, credos, and inspirational messages that plaster the walls of classrooms indicate that educators care about students. And I return from every trip to a school with virtually the same positive impression. It's a feeling of, Wow, we have a lot of caring teachers in schools! It's a special profession with many special people.

But two barriers must be crossed. The first is the cognitive bias that permeates our thinking. I've offered my best arguments on that topic already.

Powerful, caring relationships will make a difference, but so will the surrounding culture. It takes a village to raise a child, yes, but the research now informs us that culture matters in ways that could not be scientifically documented previously. The brain adapts to a variety of environmental influences. Creating a system with conditions in place that support the growth of intelligent behaviors and strengths (another way of saying we need a whole child-friendly *system*) is the next step beyond the classroom.

The evidence that the ecological approach (or what is known more typically as school climate) drives learning, by the way, continues to mount. The 2013 Gallup Student Poll, a 20-question survey that measures the hope, engagement, and well-being of students in Grades 5–12, shows clearly that these are the key factors that drive students' grades, achievement scores, retention, and future employment (www.gallupstudentpoll.com).

Eventually, this must be taken more seriously. Ecologists know how interrelationships between plants, animals, climate, and terrain result in healthy, sustainable ecosystems. Nature seems intuitively smart about these matters, and science backs up the intuition. And in perhaps the most significant achievement of modern life, the appropriate ecosystem for producing healthy human beings has been documented. Psychologists, biologists, sociologists, geneticists, neuroscientists, anthropologists, and other assorted experts draw a clear picture of how parenting, community, stress, opportunity, poverty, care, trauma, and affluence—among many other factors—nurture or retard the development of self-sustaining adults. The deep burrowing into family systems, communication patterns, personality traits, relationships, has added to the knowledge base. With a fair degree of accuracy, we can now say what's best for children, and what isn't.

That's a long way of saying that you, by yourself, are not responsible for making every student exhibit a thrive-and-drive personality. But it is possible to do your best for every child in your vicinity.

Signs of a Healthy Ecosystem

Think of the growth mindset and positive strengths as the soil for the ecosystem. In fact, with all of the evidence showing that teachers are brain changers, think of these beliefs as your core tools. With those beliefs firmly established as inner convictions, given voice through your vocabulary and interactions with students, and operationalized in your daily lessons, eight principles are sufficient to guide your work:

- *Partnering with students.* Mark Prensky (2011), game designer and advocate for educational change, calls for changing our pedagogy from "teaching by telling" to "partnering." This includes reassigning the roles of teacher and student to acknowledge two facts about the global age. First, the role of the traditional teacher has shifted to what I term *learn/teach*—the concept that each of us, regardless of age, degrees, or stature, has been rendered a learner by information abundance and rapid change. Equally, young people can now use information resources to produce *new* knowledge.

- *Starting with questions.* Teaching now starts with questions, not providing answers or expecting one right answer. This is a mindset shift, not just a strategy or technique or bell ringer activity. It requires a systematic look at the classroom as well as the school. But it's the province of passion, authenticity, and curiosity.

- *Rebalancing content and skills.* Students learn what is assessed, not always what they are taught. Assessment and evaluation must reflect a new formula for content, skills, and strengths. Students need to know how they are progressing on these critical skills, and you need to know the gaps so you can coach for success. In the next chapter, we'll look at emerging systems to help you do that.

- *Adopt a new vocabulary.* The fuzzy outlook on skills begins with the outdated vocabulary of industrial education, in which writing an essay or solving a math problem is traditionally regarded as a "hard" skill, while communicating with someone who disagrees with you or collaborating effectively in a diverse team are considered "soft" skills. This is more than a vocabulary issue. It confirms the hierarchy that gives greater weight to academic achievement and stigmatizes the teaching of skills. It also ignores a fact obvious to most adults: communication and collaboration are the most difficult of human skills—and need to be taught and practiced relentlessly (ask your partner or spouse).

- *Get that list off the wall!* Look at that list of desirable outcomes that is in the Student Handbook, on the laminated poster on the wall, or preached as a theme of the month. Integrate key strengths into your lessons and units. Use personal learning logs, journals, blogs, or other reflective means to have students record and share their progress. Make it gradable if allowed; if not, do it anyways and build intrinsic motivation and reward in your classroom.

- *Be comfortable with qualitative assessment.* Skills don't fit into our current assessment system; they can only be assessed through performance rubrics, which can be quite good (and are getting better). I offer examples of these in the Afterword of the book. Yes, rubrics are imperfect instruments that are inherently subjective, based on observation, loosely tied to letter grades, and cannot meet industrial standards of measurement. But they do quite nicely to give students direction and feedback on critical skills for work and life. Welcome to Google's world.

- *Move from "hard" to challenge.* Mastering 21st century skills demands a broader view of human functioning and new standards for performance. Outdated notions of rigor as a tensile measure (How hard can I make this test?) or quantity (How much homework can I give them?) don't tap the depths of motivation necessary to foster self-determination and awareness. Instead, detailed rubrics that describe world-class skillfulness, work ethic, habits of mind, craftsmanship, and deep thinking help students develop from *within.*

- *Link skills to purpose.* Increasingly, we face a systemic issue as we attempt to upgrade education and fit it into the global culture: We can't teach 21st century skills without *purposeful engagement.* This point relates to the above comments on hardness. Skills emerge from deep within, spurred by challenge, freedom, and meaning. In the last few years, there has been a flurry of books describing the effects of purpose, including *The Path to Purpose* by William Damon (2008) and *Drive* by Daniel Pink (2009). These and other books attest to research showing that purpose drives performance, and that purpose derives from meaningful engagement with topics that matter. Engagement, by the way, is not the same as hard work. Many students work quite hard at school, but not for reasons of intellectual mastery. Teachers sense a distancing from the material and an adherence to the rules, rather than the spirit of learning, that gives rise to cynicism. The results are often noticeable in the creative and critical abilities of students to solve problems on their own, without a formal curriculum to guide them. University professors in the United States, for example, find students know how to follow directions quite well, but have more trouble finding solutions on their own. That, too, has become a worldwide complaint.

Remember also that the ecosystem runs on assumptions that contrast directly with the deficit model of human nature, which presumes that emotions interfere with rational thinking or that young humans will tend to run wild if left unsupervised or unattended by overseers. As a parent, I'm not immune to this point of view, but the great lessons of positivity and the heart–brain pathways should lead us to a far more balanced position. Under conditions in which mastery, meaning, autonomy, and purpose drive the ecosystem, students will flourish. *Flourish*, in this context, means tapping into their unlimited potential. *Full potential* is a well-intentioned term, but assumes that adults can predict the end product. In the system we're moving toward, a child should be seen as an open system, capable of unexpected growth and greatness.

More pointedly, what is now clear about intelligence mandates educational transformation, not a "fix" or reform of the present system. Nothing will be achieved by adding another program on character education or an additional arts class. Without creating a systematic ecosystem founded on deep respect, connection, meaningful exchange, nonjudgmental actions, and affection for our youth, developing intelligent behaviors in the next generation—the "will and skill" necessary to success, in the words of Dr. Tony Wagner (2008)—will continue to be a random by-product of education, not an intended outcome.

This means letting go of "doing it better" and instead "doing it different." At first, that may not seem like a viable option. If you've been embroiled in state mandated standards, pacing guides, end-of-year exams, and high-stakes testing for the past decade, you may have either lost hope that you can change what you teach or, as I have found in conversations with younger teachers, feel inadequate when it comes to teaching without strict curriculum requirements.

But I find reasons to take heart. Below the radar of mass media, focused on test results and budget issues, a global earthquake is reshaping education. Three billion young people under the age of 25 live across the seven continents, and it has not escaped the notice of many of their teachers that old forms of education do not work. As the global community moves forward to help children expand their capabilities to meet the requirements of their world, much of educators' work will be to test and refine a set of three *principles* that will guide education forward into the next few decades. The actual shifts in curriculum requirements, testing schedules, and so forth will play out on the larger stage of society and politics. But in *your* classroom, with *your* students, in *your* community, it is absolutely possible to make your students smarter.

Moving Forward . . .

Envisioning Your Ideal Graduate

I find that educators don't need to change their mental model of education so much as allow their deeper concerns and beliefs to emerge. Virtually no teacher I meet, for example, endorses traditional standards wholeheartedly. This does not mean that they reject standards; nearly all teachers want strong guidelines for classroom instruction and recognize the value in codifying teaching objectives.

But the dissatisfaction with the information-laden curriculum is widespread. One way to test your beliefs is the following exercise. Take a blank outline of a student and impose your outcomes on the student. What do you think is critical? What qualities would you like to see students demonstrate to you? What is your ideal graduate?

Reflection Questions . . .

1. How would you rate your mentoring skills on a scale of 1 to 10? What are your strengths? Your challenges?

2. What problems or challenges do you foresee as education moves toward a more personalized system?

3. Do you feel you can help effect change—or do you feel powerless?

6 Rethink Rigor

Preparing for Deeper Learning

Imagine this scenario. All 50 states in the United States approve the Common Core State Standards and, in an unprecedented burst of transnational cooperation, 50 other countries adopt the same standards. Miraculously, the world now operates according to a single set of learning outcomes. The media report an astounding development: a resolution co-sponsored by the United States, China, and Finland has been introduced to amend the UN Charter by including the (newly named) Common Core International Standards as *the* learning goals for the 21st century. Yay! The CCIS have triumphed.

But . . . wait a minute. What now?

I think that's a pretty fair question to ask. How critical are standards to the future of education? My answer is . . . somewhat. Of course, students need to learn deep, meaningful content. Standards provide good guidelines for teachers, and do a fine job of describing middle-of-the-road information needed as a base of knowledge. They need not be perfect, either. If certain versions of local standards contain gaps (if students aren't required to learn about climate change in Wyoming or American literature in Britain, for example), the world will not fall apart. There's something called the Internet.

Moreover, it's useful to remind ourselves of the obvious: middle school and high school teachers aren't teaching grad school–level rocket science, and the same subjects have been taught for nearly 100 years. By now, a competent teacher pretty much knows what to deliver to people under the age of 18. With the bulk of teachers, it's entirely reasonable to put some guidelines and expectations in place, and let them get on with it.

So why the obsessive conversation about standards that currently preoccupies the western world? First, at the center of this heated debate lies a presumption: if just the right standards can be encoded into education, things will settle down. Every student will learn exactly what he or she needs to know. The formula will be complete.

The second reason is closely related to ideas in this book: maybe the new standards can be used to drive deeper learning, critical thinking, and problem solving. Can they? I think we'll find out that standards can light the path, but they won't get us to our destination.

WHY STANDARDS AREN'T THE "IT"

The impulse of the writers of the Common Core State Standards in the United States, surely shared by even those who disagree with specifics, is a noble one: to find an antidote to the narrow test-based accountability and laundry list of outcomes spawned by the No Child Left Behind legislation of the 2000s. By that measure, the Common Core is a healthy alternative. This comment applies also to the Next Generation Science Standards now making their way into classrooms, as well as other efforts worldwide to update guidelines for 21st century learning.

The new standards are less than perfect, as most everyone agrees (although we don't know how imperfect since they haven't been carefully piloted). They tend to be verbose, "committee generated" paragraphs that can be "murky" or "indecipherable" (Schmoker 2014). They retain too much from the old standards as well. I spoke last spring with a very capable, committed, and knowledgeable 10th grade geometry teacher about the Common Core State Standards (CCSS) for Mathematics. He laughed when I asked him about several of the new priority standards. "I don't know why they need to know this," he said of his students.

That's a problem. If we don't know why we're teaching it, you can be sure the students don't know why they're learning it.

The Deeper Challenge

But the real dilemma dare not be named: intuitively, we know the fundamental balance between process and information is shifting in favor of a new mental skill set that replaces the cumulative acquisition of knowledge. The existing formula of establishing content, prescribing content, and testing for acquisition of content no longer applies.

For starters, every day there is less standardization of information, making it nearly impossible to decide what a fifth grader or 10th grader should know. Beyond the core literacies of reading, writing, computation, and research, the worldwide culture of innovation, discovery, multipolarity, interdisciplinary thinking, and rapid change depends on the explosive potential of the human mind, not entombed truths from the past.

Increasingly, any standards-based curriculum is at odds with the outside world. A standard curriculum treats reality as if it is fixed, rarely referencing the momentous scientific breakthroughs and general upending of known truths likely to occur in the next 50 years. There is no guarantee—in fact, there is every opposite indicator—that the knowledge of today will survive. The global community is reinventing information. One hundred years from now, standards, if they exist at all, may be completely unrecognizable (Hall, 2013).

But what to do now? How do we honor content, but shift to a skills and attitude curriculum? One challenge, as observers point out, "is that we don't yet know how to teach self-direction, collaboration, creativity, and innovation the way we know how to teach long division" (Rotherham & Willingham, 2009). More skills instruction also mandates letting go of content—and this is another sticking point. Should students be required to enroll in calculus? How much literature should they read? What book list do we choose? That conversation surfaces the real elephant in the room: These days, what does a learned person need to "know" to qualify as a lifelong learner? The Google employees may rely on attitude, but they arrive with a fund of information, facts, and concepts embedded somewhere in their brains—a fund that grows through collaboration and technology. But what's the starting point?

Do Better Standards Mean Smarter Students?

Despite our recognition that the world is transforming, content, information, and subject mastery still reign in the minds of the public, teachers, and students as signs of excellence. While trying to find some diversion from the task of writing this chapter, I looked at the daily digest of educational news. The lead story announced that yet another American high school has decided to offer a broader range of Advanced Placement courses to more students. (For non-U.S. readers, Advanced Placement, or AP, is a program created by the College Board that offers college-level curriculum and examinations to high school students.) The school adopted the approach based on a highly successful program in a Portland, Oregon, school district that moved it from one of the bottom 10 districts in that state to one of the top 10 districts in the United States, according to *Newsweek* magazine.

I'll resist taking a swipe at a popular magazine that annually confuses the public by ranking the quality of high schools by test scores, SAT results, and other outdated industrial benchmarks (Google staff may also have opinions on this). And, in fairness, I want to note that the principal who announced the rationale for more AP courses cited the chief reason behind the decision as helping students develop more "grit" (McKibbin, 2014).

Actually, in that last statement, there are clues to the internal crosscurrents underlying the discussion on standards. The strange fact is that no one is very happy. Like the gap between the value of an official currency and the black market value, standards sail along as if unanimity rules. But around the world, I find considerable unease. A young English teacher in Canada said to me recently, "Standards are like a straightjacket. They keep our students from really learning."

Beyond the sense that standards encourage a one-size-fits-all mentality, or are at odds with a world that increasingly values creativity and innovation, there is a deeper concern that the standards approach, rather than making students smarter, reinforces the notion of lifeless information fed into the minds of students (Thomas, 2010). That's backed up by current findings in neuroplasticity, which punches daily holes in the notion of a fixed brain apparatus that prefers to take in information rather than construct it. It's possible, in fact, looking at the new research on brain development, to speculate that our methods actually do narrow pathways and make students *dumber*.

Can We Rebalance Knowing and Doing?

Attempting to codify knowledge by writing an extensive list of standards that contain application and problem-solving requirements does more than simply repackage the present system. Though the new standards are rooted in the same subjects and curricular approaches popular for over 100 years, they do attempt to do it better.

That will not prove sufficient. As Mark Prensky (2011), game-based learning expert, educational critic, and author of *The Five Skills Framework*, puts it, "What the reformers haven't yet understood is that it's not the "system" that we need to get right; *it's the education that the system provides*."

For that reason, the topic of standards, school transformation, and teaching skills can't be divided. At the core of the noisy debate over standards is our vision of school itself: How do schools transition from an information-scarce world to a process-personalized world with on-demand information and shifting environmental constraints?

Partly, of course, the answer is in teaching the new standards better. The Common Core standards demand pedagogical shifts that focus on complexity, application, and deep understanding (EngageNY, n.d.). This is a positive turn and in the eyes of some observers, "can and should serve as a unique transformational opportunity for our nation's teaching and learning systems" (Kay & Lenz, n.d.). But grave doubts exist about whether the teaching force can adapt.

Let's consider revering the equation: Can standards be adapted to great teachers? Once we move past standards as primary, fixed, and obligatory, the real conversation about redesigning education—the dialogue that will determine (and I mean this literally) whether our civilization stands or falls—can begin. That conversation should be furious, hot and heavy, and full of as much creative fire as we can muster. Instead of trying to codify information from past centuries, we better be looking at how students will handle the incoming flow of traffic. In my view, the current debate over standards is a sign of ignorance, not enlightenment. It consumes us, but offers empty calories, not sustenance for a deeper and longer journey.

RESETTING THE BAR: PERSONAL RIGOR

The chief barrier to moving forward is an outdated definition of *rigor*. The core task of the modern world is not to prep students for standardized tests by delivering content, or even to make them "college ready," but to prepare them to judge the quality of information, generate new ideas, filter them through a net of critical analysis and reflection, and share and move the ideas through a design process to create a quality product, either as an idea or a material object.

This process asks more of students than just thinking and problem solving. As an example, in his book, Prensky (2011) identifies five skills that should be part of a standard-based curriculum: figuring out the right thing to do, getting it done, working with others, doing it creatively, and continually doing it better. These are deep processes that require flexible minds, agile inquiry, and intuitive behaviors from students, as well as the application of 21st century skills such as communication, collaboration, critical thinking, and creativity—the four Cs which have lately entered the vocabulary of education.

So far, education has focused on ways to evoke these skills. Incorporating voice and choice, crafting personalized environments, and honoring the growth mindset are examples of viable strategies that increase intelligent behaviors. But they do no good unless accompanied by a new standard for performance that makes skillful behavior and attitude the foundation for assessment, meaning teachers need to find ways to *standardize and assess* those behaviors and skills. Once clear on the outcomes, we can backward map to figure out how to teach them. That's the design issue, really.

Skills versus Strengths

What might a standard for personal rigor look like? First, let's distinguish skills from strengths. Skills can be taught, demonstrated, and measured through performance evaluations. However, skillful performance depends on attitude and intelligent behaviors that cannot be directly taught, but must be evoked through purposeful engagement fueled by meaningful challenge.

For example, successful collaboration relies on intangibles such as empathy, openness, and flexibility (the humility factor, in Google's world). Success is fueled by inspiration, openness, metacognition, and deep thinking inside the black box of the brain, which then manifest as visible competencies.

So, the first step in visioning and assessing personal rigor: *skills and strengths differ.* It's a crucial distinction because attitude is a hidden virtue, surfaced through reflection, conversation, and interaction; attitude emerges under the right conditions. It can only be assessed through qualitative means, while skillful behavior can be described in a performance rubric. The fact that these lists often sit side by side, or even been merged, is a legacy of the cognitive paradigm. In education, everything has been turned into a *skill.* For example, global awareness, which often makes either list, is regarded as a skill instead of an attitude or state of mind. The default is understandable. A skill can be assessed; an attitude evades our instruments and takes us out of our zone of comfort.

Making the Four Cs Central to Instruction

The good news is that personal rigor has begun to enter the vocabulary of education through the relatively recent introduction of the four Cs. The essential step now is to incorporate these skills into daily classroom work by intentionally teaching and assessing these skills, using world-class rubrics that are more than adequate for the task. (To view samples, see the resources in the Afterword for rubrics that can be downloaded for your use.)

Even with 15% of the 21st century gone, the notion of teaching skills meets resistance. Presented with the idea, a Maryland teacher once responded to me with an angry comment: "We can't teach these," she exclaimed. "There's no place in the grade book for it!" And, yes, technically she was on firm ground. But many schools I work with have found ways to make skillful behavior up to 40% of the grade. The rebalancing has to include assessment; 21st century skills acquisition cannot be an add-on or afterthought.

A host of other issues surface when teaching and assessing skills, most of which I will explore in depth in the remainder of the book. Skills and strengths respond to mentoring rather than teaching, require new methods for scaffolding, and invoke different levels of depth. Teaching students to collaborate in teams, for example, is easier than eliciting creativity. But the overall message, as you will read, is that skills and strengths can be integrated into the fabric of the teaching day, be made highly visible and important as outcomes, and become the foundation for powerful practices that lead to better cognitive outcomes.

The Fifth C

Recent books have made us aware of how schools turned into institutions in which intelligent behaviors become secondary to learning content. In his introduction to *How Children Succeed*, author Paul Tough (2012) notes that the rise of the cognitive hypothesis—the belief that success depends primarily on the kind of intelligence measured by IQ tests and relentless, early practice of the associated cognitive skills—can be traced to very recent origins.

In fact, the conversation took root in 1994 when reports showed that children were not receiving sufficient cognitive stimulation in the first three years of life, and so arrived in kindergarten unready to learn. Thus began the incessant march toward a neat, linear, input/output model of learning and the final split between child development and education. Intellect became the prize; more subtle aspects of human personality, such as persistence, self-control, curiosity, conscientiousness, grit, and self-confidence, were left by the wayside.

Though *noncognitive* may remain embedded in the vocabulary of education, the term is on the verge of obsolescence (Wagner, 2006). Too much evidence has accumulated showing that character strengths, motivation issues, conscientiousness, self-control, and other psychological capabilities are at play in intelligence and achievement. These are the intelligent behaviors, which can also be considered a sign of *character.* For that reason, I often call intelligent behaviors the fifth C.

It's a big word. How do we teach character without turning school into a therapy session? Actually, it's surprisingly easy. There is no need to associate character attributes with moral or religious movements. Character can be defined as a set of abilities of strengths that are malleable and can be learned (Peterson & Seligman, 2004). In other words, they are intelligent or resilient behaviors. They may be deep and mysterious, but the great advantage of a personalized, inquiry-based approach to learning, which relies on connection, communication, and a positive culture to bring out the best in students, is that character becomes much more visible than when students sit in neat rows and receive information from the front of the room while remaining well behaved. In the midst of problem solving, character emerges. In a thrive-and-drive classroom, it flourishes.

You can't teach character, any more than you can teach someone to drive a car by reading the manual. Nor can the behaviors be graded. And judgment cuts the process short, surely the reason so many students disengage from learning. But they grow in the presence of a supportive environment, authentic challenge, appreciative inquiry, kind feedback, meaningful purpose and accomplishment, and close contact with a teacher who cares, and who models the same strengths.

CAN WE ASSESS THE WHOLE CHILD?

Deepening assessment practices as the new global standard begins to revolve around inquiry and personal competencies is a necessity. How we get there will be a steady conversation through the next decade. But it is possible to assess the whole child.

First, the new form of rigor is not a content-free zone. The industrial system of learning has aided many young people in becoming educated, over many decades, and many aspects of that model will endure. It's quite difficult to say with precision what educated people know, but it's like art—it's recognizable, and we value it. Students need information, facts, and specific knowledge for a successful outcome. Students with a deeper knowledge base do well in school, but also bring that prior knowledge to bear when solving problems or analyzing novel events. The goal is to blend the content and the skills into a seamless package.

First, that means that testing, even through multiple choice exams, will and should endure. Second, the difference between skills and strengths needs to be recognized—and assessed accordingly. Third, the 21st century skills themselves should be differentiated. The visible skills—collaboration and communication—can be assessed against a performance standard, using a rubric. Critical thinking and creativity are the result of a *deep* process, closer to strengths and intelligent behaviors than skills, and must be assessed more qualitatively. And a final consideration: the entire inquiry process cannot be assessed without deep listening, debating, and other tools of formative assessment (Heitin, 2014).

Your most immediate tools are performance rubrics. There is no alternative route to 21st century assessment. (I list available resources for world-class rubrics in the Afterword.) This is partly a responsibility of individual teachers, but every school should develop schoolwide rubrics used consistently by all teachers. At a minimum, schools should consider a schoolwide rubric for teamwork and collaboration (the foundational skill for 21st century learning) and communication and presentation (which includes facilitation and speaking skills that encourage intelligent behaviors and personal competencies). To get at character and work habits, your most powerful tool is a work ethic performance rubric, which can be adapted to measure behaviors in the classroom and a training tool for younger students learning to develop their personal strengths (see the Afterword for details on how to download this rubric).

In all of this, the old tendency is to see assessment as a tool; in inquiry, it's a process that depends in large part on a relationship-driven system of teaching in which assessment and learning can't easily be distinguished. You're talking with students and, at the same time, finding out what they know and how you can help them (Schwartz, 2014d).

USING PROJECT-BASED INQUIRY: THE DEEPER LEARNING MODEL

Let's first agree on priorities. Figuring out how schools systematically teach and assess the "it" factor should preoccupy us. In a very real sense, the defining challenge for teachers is to disband the standard school model and craft a more contemporary set of outcomes for students. The outline of this new system is surprisingly clear, with global unanimity, as reflected in the many consensus reports on reinventing schooling (Leadbeater & Wong, 2010). Most forecasts center on four core principles: (1) Children become protagonists in learning, not recipients; (2) learning is collaborative, including teacher to student and peer to peer; (3) learning is more clearly related to real-world questions and problems; and (4) teachers shift from broadcasters to facilitators.

The details will emerge, but ahead lies a skills-based, collaborative, inquiry-driven, learner-centered system of teaching and learning. In that system, information will not be king, tests scores will not rule the airwaves, and standards will be reduced to minimal guidelines that acknowledge the dynamics of knowledge in a co-creative, constructed world. Information must still be gathered during the process of creation, but in a usable, just in time format not found in "subjects."

But the move to inquiry does not mean that the Montessori system will take over high schools. For young children, discovery is appropriate play; for older students, intellectual guidance is a necessity. That is why the research into discovery learning has reported quite negative results (Kirschner, Sweller, & Clark, 2010). The goal is not complete freedom for students, but a deep learning relationship between partners.

It does mean, however, that content standards, no matter how cleverly written, cannot be the guiding force around which education in the future is constructed. There's too much on-demand, online, networked, Internet of Everything information floating around. In a force field like this, standards feel limited and archaic the moment they're printed.

Teachers already feel this way. I see it in their eyes and nodding agreement, in their commitment to finding something deeper for their students, in their desire to serve their profession better. They know something is afoot; they just don't how to describe it.

At the same time, it is possible to align teaching with standards and still offer a support and incentive system that develops and supports the "it" factor. A first step is to move away from the laundry list of standards, create a culture of inquiry in schools, and keep our eyes on the prize: A full-on, problem-solving system in which the core outcome is to help student learn to think, collaborate, communicate, and *feel*. I emphasize the latter because solving problems, especially in the context of creativity and innovation, is a whole-body exercise. Part of passing through the portal into the future is the ultimate recognition that resiliency, empathy, purpose, and commitment to causes beyond the self must be engraved into the system.

The Deeper Learning Model

One place to start is to align your school or classroom with the evolving model of deeper learning, a movement that incorporates elements of great teaching with the need to teach skills and strengths (Schwartz, 2014a). The model recognizes the importance of mastering content, so it fits with a standards-based environment. But it adds five additional competencies: critical thinking, effective oral and written communication, collaboration, learning how to learn, and developing academic mindsets.

It's vital to restate that content is not the sole measure; the other competencies receive equal treatment (this impacts the grading system in many schools). The concepts work together in harmony, integrated into a unified system of teaching, learning, and assessment. It often results in exhibitions of learning in which student simultaneously demonstrate their skills and content acquisition, as well as reflection. Bob Lenz, CEO of Envision Schools and a thought leader for the model, says it this way: "[M]ost schools and most of our learning stops at knowing and we need to move that and broaden it to the doing and reflecting" (Schwartz, 2014d).

The last competency—developing a 21st century academic mindset—is of critical importance to fulfilling that goal. It is the mindset of inquiry, joyful accomplishment, self-improvement, and deep curiosity, all fueled by a supportive teacher in a mentor and coaching role who can guide, assess, and encourage. And it begins where I started: with the core conditions that create a thrive, drive, and flourish environment, in which students engage fully in the innately satisfying task of learning.

What fuels the mindset? In the views of deeper learning advocates, the four factors will sound familiar to readers of this book:

- *Belonging to an academic community.* Feeling connected to adults and peers at school intellectually, not just socially.
- *Belief in the likelihood of success.* As research shows, belief in one's own self-efficacy is a better predictor of academic success than measured ability.
- *The work has meaning and value.* The brain naturally looks for connections. Relevance and authenticity count for everything.
- *Beliefs that abilities and intelligence can grow with effort.* This is the "growth mindset" so essential to today's life. This is the area in which challenge, growth, mastery, and joy converge.

Using Project-Based Inquiry

The deeper learning model is usually associated with a project-based instructional model (project-based learning, or PBL). PBL is an organized, accountable, engaging method for leading students through a multi-week, problem-solving process centered on an open-ended, authentic question. It invokes all the goals and attributes of the deeper learning model into an instructional design, including a focus attention on the skills and strengths necessary for successful inquiry (for that reason, I prefer the term *project-based inquiry*).

For teachers interested in mastering PBL, I recommend a number of resources in the Resources Section, including my earlier book, *The Project Based Learning Design and Coaching Guide* (2012).

PBL is not the only way for teaching the new personal rigor, however. Rather than serving as an instructional strategy, PBL takes students through a "deep dive" experience in which they must use their skills and strengths to succeed. Those skills and strengths must be continually addressed in daily classroom activities and consistently modeled when students and teachers interact, regardless of the lesson.

Obviously, life teaches many of these necessary lessons for developing character, but it would not be complete without adult guidance. This is the coaching role discussed in the next chapter. Teachers who talk *at,* rather than talk *with,* students have generally not been successful in any environment. But in a connected, collaborative environment focused on developing skillful behaviors, coaching assumes new prominence. As a teacher, you are now a brain-changer, capable of influencing outlook and thinking patterns.

Moving Forward . . .

Taking Charge of Standards

If you're a teacher who feels the tension between mandated standards and good teaching, you might be looking for a "Monday morning solution" to the standards question. What is your personal stance toward standards, and how do you approach them? Do you see standards as written in stone or received truth? Or do you filter standards through your own sensibilities and teaching expertise? Do you trust yourself to make good judgments for your students? What else can you do to personalize your teaching in an era in which standards still rule? Here are three ideas for taking charge of standards.

(Continued)

(Continued)

1. ***Treat standards as "best guess" guidelines.*** Since standards serve a purpose, they won't disappear overnight. But let's treat them from now on as if they represent a compendium of the best thinking of the human race about what it was important to know *last year*. Use them as a platform, a guideline, a reference for lesson planning, and a slightly flawed measure of what we hope students will know in the future. As a teacher, decide what is non-negotiable, and teach that content. Other than that, breathe. The Monday morning solution? Include a "breakthrough" column on every rubric that offers students the open space to filter the standards through their own thinking and create original answers to authentic issues (and every lesson should have an authentic context).

2. ***Think in terms of "personal rigor."*** Now it gets harder. In a system measured by mastery of process, what defines a scholar? How do we affirm excellence? What is the slimmed down version of essential knowledge in a Google world? In essence, how do we move from content mastery to *personal rigor*—a kind of ready-for-the-world pose characterized by confidence, resiliency, curiosity, openness, and the ability to track down and integrate the information and skills necessary for competency in one's life and work? The obvious first step? Minimize testing and stop obsessing over cognitive skills. A second step is to admit a great truth about the world: we *don't know* exactly what the scholar of the future looks like. So let's use deep, well-constructed performance rubrics that honor the whole child, assess growth in attitude and thinking skills as well as content, and allow children to inform us about their future.

3. ***Teach a "forward-leaning" curriculum.*** Alfred North Whitehead said it well in 1916: *"The secondhandedness of the learned world is the secret of its mediocrity."* Moving to first-hand grappling with the intellectual and social issues of the day is now a paramount goal. If we're teaching to nurture inquiry, we can't teach to the test alone. Nor, in the face of evidence that a degree by itself is not sufficient, can college be held up as the carrot to drive performance. To liberate the purposeful behavior required to fuel deeper learning, students will need a compelling reason to engage content. The Monday morning solution? As much as possible, organize instruction around service and issues that matter to the future of young people. Don't start with standards; start with what matters, and then fit the standards into instruction—carefully.

4. ***Use a MOOC to learn about the "deeper learning" model.*** The deeper learning website maintains an excellent array of resources, including an online course on deeper learning (dlmooc.deeper-learning.org).

Reflection Questions . . .

1. Is it possible to teach the standards without becoming standardized? How do you do it?

2. How would you grade personal rigor?

3. If you haven't tried project-based leanring as a teaching method, why?

7 Be a Co-Learner
Coaching Intelligent Behaviors

Becoming a coach and mentor doesn't mean that lecture is dead, instruction passé, or content disappeared. Though the teacher's role is shifting dramatically from distributor of information to helping students research, curate, and create products as they process information, the era of the content expert is not over. In fact, the opposite. You won't spend as much time delivering information from the front of the room, but you will need to offer a context for learning and respond to students' on-demand inquiries and questions. That demands deep expertise in your subject. But your knowledge will be shared by speaking one on one, conducting small workshops on topics of student interest, and filling gaps on the fly as students engage in inquiry, hit speed bumps, and ask for help.

In other words, you remain a teacher in the traditional sense, but now must integrate coaching into your daily routines. That requires that you shift the mental model of your job. Given the daily barrage of messages focused on classroom management, discipline, delivery methods, intervention strategies, and other hallmarks of front-of-the-room instruction, this isn't easy. How do you reinvent yourself?

REDEFINING YOUR ROLE

Think first of what coaches do. Coaches are employed to help people become more skillful, versatile, and capable. This sounds similar to what teachers also do, but with one critical difference: teachers convey information, while coaches use information to equip people to guide themselves. Coaches may act as teachers on occasion, but they know that skills come out of a catalytic process, not direct instruction. They also know that knowledge alone doesn't make a student competent; thoughts, intentions, emotions, and perspective matter more.

Thus, a first step is to think broadly about your new mission. Outside of education, coaching is a well-developed profession, with best practices for relating, facilitating, assessing, and conversing. Coaches have specific objectives in mind, as listed in *Leader as Coach,* by David Peterson and Mary Hicks (2010):

1. *Forge a partnership.* Build trust and understanding so people want to work with you.

2. *Inspire commitment.* Build motivation so people focus on goals that matter.

3. *Grow skills.* Build competencies so people know how to do what's required.

4. *Promote persistence.* Build stamina and discipline so learning lasts.

5. *Shape the environment.* Build in supports to reward learning and remove barriers to learning.

This list doesn't sound so different from good teaching—so what's the difference? It's a big one: any one of these coaching strategies begins with the person—not the test or curriculum. In fact, the foundation of successful coaching is respect for individual choice and the rock-solid belief that every person is entitled to that choice. Coaching begins with dignity and worth, not a list of prescribed objectives and automatic sanctions. Coaching and instructional mandates don't easily mix, so you will need an additional skill: knowing when to coach and when to use traditional delivery methods to focus on curriculum requirements and push students to move forward.

Knowing When and Why to Lecture

Grant Wiggins (2014b), originator of *Understanding by Design,* offers a series of three articles which offer good guidelines for lecturing. The good news first: lectures can be effective for certain purposes, such as modeling thought processes, sharing cognitive structures, giving context, or telling stories that draw students into the topic.

The downside is better known: lectures are as effective as other methods for transmitting information, but entirely unsuited for promoting thought, developing values, or changing attitudes. They run completely counter to what is known about the efficacy of formative assessment, high-level questioning and discussion, and metacognition. Add to that the fact that most lecturers are prone to self-deception ("I can't be *that* boring").

But nontraditional forms of lecture, such as flipped classrooms, can be very effective if they incorporate the coaching mentality and encourage active exchange with students by beginning with a question, making attempts to help students understand the significance of the content, stimulating students to engage in critical judgment, making an argument about how to answer the question, and ending with questions.

Of course, sometimes during coaching you run into a wall of misunderstanding or lack of basic knowledge. What to do at that point? Offer a "just in time" lecture. It won't hurt.

PURPOSEFUL COACHING

It's a strange fact, but establishing good relationships with students runs counter to tradition. This is not so much neglect as it is a legacy of the industrial system, in which the transmission model of learning sufficed. Relationships were treated as a kind of static that interfered with the transmission. A teacher once recounted to me the speech given by the dean at his graduation from the School of Education. The dean's strongly worded advice? *Never* get to know your students. Stay distant, deliver information, and go home. That was 1965. It's a new world.

Nowadays, it's considered important to get along well with students. But the importance of establishing and maintaining good relationships is usually pitched as a *classroom strategy,* a means to create an orderly learning environment and control over the process of learning. It's a disciplinary technique, not a basis for coaching young people to perform at their best.

Two shifts in the landscape, one scientific and the other cultural, have disrupted this model. First, neuroscience tells us that attending to the emotional states of students is our first option for better performance. Knowing your students well and crafting a positive relationship with them allows you as the teacher to gauge and adjust, offer scaffolds, or model behaviors that calm or reassure students. Attitude matters more than we knew. Diminishing stress or creating a happy mood through your own behavior allows students to function at a reasonable level and get the work of school done.

Thus, a first breakthrough is to recognize the centrality of relationships in today's classrooms. It's known already that positive relationships key and calibrate recall of knowledge and ability to attend to the tasks of school (Pillars, 2012). As school climate studies generally show, positive relationships raise student achievement levels.

And, for academic outcomes, a positive climate is sufficient. But as you've read, intelligent behaviors such as critical inquiry, creativity, innovative and design thinking, deep collaboration, and the kind of self-managing, entrepreneurial growth mindset required in the world that can't really be taught, at least not like a "normal" skill. There's no pacing guide for creativity.

The short story? As education moves toward more personalized, inquiry-based approaches dependent on a student's inner resolve, curiosity, and openness, it won't be enough to settle for happy classrooms or surveys showing high student engagement. The teacher–student bond will need to be informed by a higher purpose and the intentional goals of establishing relationships that offer each student the maximum opportunity to develop a thrive-and-drive mentality. That is how I define the term *purposeful coaching.* It is our best effort to help young people discover, reflect on, and demonstrate new expressions of intelligence.

The new strengths and skills don't respond to the "coach and correct" approach to relationships, either. The great cultural shift toward making the inner life more visible at work and play is forcing us to recognize that the intelligent behaviors qualities vital to success are immune to old techniques of teaching and coaching. The intelligent behaviors now valued in today's world can be evoked by coaching, but not taught.

Purposeful coaching requires coaching tools and techniques, as described in the last section of this chapter. But now I would ask you to consider again the themes in the Preface and Chapter 1. The shift from teacher to purposeful coach is personal; the tools matter less than how you show up in your inter-actions with your students. This is your coaching *presence,* a combination of your personality, beliefs, and communication style.

Social neuroscience and studies of the heart tells us that coaching pres-ence has two-way implications. What attitude do you bring to the exchange? Do you approach with the belief or feeling that this student will be uncooper-ative or can't be coached, or do you radiate a kind of benevolence that invites empathy? What do students experience when you coach them? Do they feel "open" or resistant? Do you inspire or constrain? And how do you react when feeling frustrated or thwarted, despite your best intentions?

The bottom line is that no tool will be of much benefit if you can't adopt the sympathetic view necessary to connect with the inner life of students and tap the deep wells of intelligence within them. Your presence is the founda-tion for successful coaching. And though it might be a disconcerting fact to Schools of Education focused on teaching techniques to prospective teachers, your presence can't really be taught, either. It must be learned—by you.

BRINGING YOUR BEST TO THE TABLE

The formula for a successful coaching presence sounds simple, but simple statements about human behavior usually hide profound truths and challenge deep beliefs and ways of being. Purposeful coaching is no exception. It relies on mastering the oldest of human frailties: unconditional acceptance.

I'll resist using the term *unconditional love,* since education tries to avoid such terminology, but that's what we're talking about. Your coaching presence will be most successful if you bring to the interaction as much care, empathy, respect, acceptance, appreciation, sense of freedom, willingness, and sense of shared destiny as you can. This is the ultimate role as the co-learner. Essentially, you convey to a student: yes, I'm older, wiser, and more knowledgeable than you are, but as human beings, we're equal. Plus, I don't know everything.

The co-learner role helps you remain open, a prerequisite for connected communication. Entering into a dialogue with students starts with an empathetic impulse often spurred by a shared sense that neither student nor teacher has all the answers—and an attitude of openness is perceived by students as a form of care. In fact, the global information age creates a Zen-like, counterintuitive reality for teachers: your greatest strength now is not what you know, but your willingness to admit what you don't know.

It is also the case that the openness you communicate to students may be the single best predictor of successful learning in the 21st century. As evidence, in *Visible Learning,* John Hattie's (2009) seminal meta-study of 800 different influences on student achievement, he cites openness as the key personality disposition and most important factor leading to intellectual engagement, self-confidence, and investment in the process of learning. Think here of neuroplasticity, the growth mindset, and the impact of sincere communication. Can openness be taught? Probably not. But can it be modeled, and thus modify behavior? Most certainly.

The Value of Appreciation

Openness goes hand in hand with *appreciative inquiry,* an approach that allows you to take your coaching from support to action. In this approach, you move into a no-fault conversation and look for strengths, positives, and possibilities. Built on the principles of positive psychology, appreciative inquiry helps students focus on next steps for change and growth. That's good. But the greater benefit is the reinforcement of psychological shifts in students that take physiological root in the body and lead to hope, greater engagement, and creativity. The connection between your attitude and intelligent behaviors is direct, immediate, and—over time—visible to you and the student.

Too much care and unconditional acceptance is never an issue in coaching, but "over-caring" can be. As we all know, there are limitations inherent in trying to help another person to change or be more intelligent. So, to unconditional care, I would add clarity as a requirement for a successful coaching presence.

Remember that changing the student is not the objective. Instead, focus on generating trust, which opens a channel of communication that conveys your curiosity, appreciation, and willingness to listen in ways that the message will be received. Once heard, the message itself does the work. I call this the *ping* factor (Markham, 2012). A ping is a network tool that sends a message from one computer to another in order to check whether it is reachable and active. If it is, it sends back a "pong" that establishes a line of communication between the computers.

Similarly, your attitude of care penetrates deep within, pointing students to their own resources, building their sense of autonomy, and resonating with their innate creativity and desire for purpose and meaning. Through purposeful coaching, you help students build their own asset base, empowering them by intentionally not trying to mold them. The channel of trust also operates both ways. They open up to you. From that point forward, it's up to the student to grow on his or her own. But the foundation is in place.

Making the Shift to a New Role

The lexicon of teacher skills rarely addresses how to facilitate student growth in a learner-centered, inquiry-based environment. It's overdue to fill that gap, so what will personalized classrooms demand of teachers? In general, competent teachers who want to skillfully lead the classrooms of the future should expect the following of themselves:

- **Shift from *classroom management* to *people management.*** Looking out over the class and maintaining order and discipline is job one in industrial classrooms. But in an inquiry-based, student-focused environment, the job gets done through norms, conversation, peer culture, and shared commitment to high performance. This doesn't mean a teacher yields control of the class. But the ability to move seamlessly into one-on-one conversation, facilitate small groups or workshops to address personalized needs of students, or even the willingness and capability to confront tears or anger, become part of the job.

  This may not be part of your original agenda when you decided to teach, or an element in your training. Earlier, I mentioned the English teacher who reacted indignantly to my suggestion that teaching now includes counselor skills. Pursed lips at the thought of having to engage students personally are not uncommon. But the same challenge applies to managers in the workplace responsible for helping others develop positive intrinsic behaviors and self-management skills.

- **Develop a personal style that** *evokes, not provokes.* There are different images of what constitutes good coaching. A "tell and sell" model has been popular in schools or, as it is sometimes called, the *amoeba theory.* To change behavior, you can either poke the organism so it moves away from you, or you put out some sugar and entice the organism in your direction. This is the behaviorist model, the core tool of the industrial classroom. It's a model that emphasizes rewards over self-motivation, eliminates self-correction, habituates actions only when there is a stimulus, and crushes long-term ambition in favor of immediate cessation of pain or immediate acquisition of the reward.

  In today's environment, with greater equality between young and old, and without automatic respect conferred on elders, telling and forcing have reached their limits of persuasion. Intelligent behaviors flourish in the presence of facilitated, respectful communication and connection. This applies to the training of teachers as well, as you may have experienced yourself. As the authors of *Evocative Coaching* remind us, when coached, teachers don't resist change; they resist *being changed* (Tschannen-Moran & Tschannen-Moran, 2010). So do students.

  It's helpful also to revisit the idea of respectful communication, particularly in light of what we now know about the brain and heart. Authors Andrew Newberg and Mark Waldman (2012) have pointed out that words have impact on the body and can build trust, resolve conflict, or increase intimacy—or not. A coach's objective is stimulate neural resonance, an empathetic state of mind, and to bring students into alignment with our goals, values, and thinking by expressing appreciation, speaking warmly and briefly, and listening deeply, for example.

- **Distinguish coach from counselor.** This is the "skill versus will" question. A coach is interested in the performance of students and helping improve that performance through coaching behaviors. But not all students are equally skilled or motivated. If a student makes a choice not to perform, then your role shifts into a counselor. In this role, you may need to be more directive and straightforward, and outline your expectations for an immediate behavior change.

- **Develop your personal "growth mindset."** A coach's role implies a willingness to get better at the job. Beyond the current vision of what constitutes a high-quality teacher lies a fresh mental model that has nothing to do with test scores, competencies, strategies, or supervisorial judgments. It's about how you view yourself in relation to your profession—and how you develop the qualities and mindset that empower you to inspire, motivate, and lead your students. Art Costa, author of *Cognitive Coaching,* refers to these qualities as dispositions or states of mind (Costa & Garmston, 2002). In his view, the human need for efficacy (including identity, competence, mastery, and self-empowerment); consciousness (to reflect on one's thoughts and actions); flexibility (the desire to adapt and change); craftsmanship (the urge to be clearer, more precise, and integrated); and interdependence (to grow in relationship to others and be social beings) represent the core internal thought processes that define true teacher expertise and lead to a wiser, more attuned, and proactive teacher.

The combination of connected communication, heartfelt exchange, and co-learning through inquiry tells us that that this mindset is transmitted to your students, visible at some level to them, and able to influence their thinking. This exchange occurs in the presence of rapport and high conversational quality. Rapport is part technique, part attitude, part observation, and part *knowledge of self.* Thus, the fastest way to understand your students is to explore your own attitudes, passions, and personality drivers. As antiquated as it might sound, education in the future will force a return to the old wisdom of *know thyself.* As you coach others, you are also coaching yourself—and vice versa.

STARTING SIMPLE

Once you're clear on your new role, a few simple coaching practices drawn from a previous book on project-based learning can help you be successful (Markham, 2012). Coaching is difficult work, in that other humans of any age will test your patience, judgment, and resolve. Think of the practices as principles, not tools. They represent parts of a process, not a set of wrenches or a hammer. A process can take time—or go wrong. In fact, it's likely you will come away from some interactions with students feeling as if nothing much successful has occurred—or maybe it went *all* wrong.

No worries. Go back to the principles. One interaction does not define you as a coach, and your good intentions alone have power. And if eliciting the deep intelligent behaviors important to education were easy, coaching would have replaced industrial education many decades ago. It's much easier to teach and test than help a young person uncover their strengths.

Principle 1: Be fully present.

If you are distracted, the coaching relationship will suffer. But the schedule typically doesn't allow for sufficient coaching time. If you use a pacing guide, plan for process time during the period and, as much as you can, rebalance your teaching to include more talk and less content (the new trends of the flipped classroom and blended learning will help immensely here). When actually sitting with students, bring personal rigor to the interaction. Breathe into your time constraints in the classroom, blot out the reality that other students are waiting expectantly for your attention, and focus on good eye contact and sincerity. Take time to listen, not tell. Better to shorten the time period of the coaching interaction, but do it well. Other items on your checklist:

- *Are you listening—or waiting to respond?* If the coaching session begins to fail, first check your listening skills. Often we seem to be listening, but are really waiting for the opportunity to advise.
- *Be aware of your Circle of Control.* A coach can improve performance by offering specific suggestions. But the bumper sticker philosophy applies: "A mind is like a parachute. It only works when it's open." If a student rejects coaching, move away and allow for natural consequences. Those also change behavior.
- *Lower emotional barriers.* Good coaches know that negative emotions block communication. To unblock, practice sincere listening and communication. If you sense that you've hit an emotional hot spot during a coaching conversation, return to listening and asking, rather than telling or advising.
- *When possible, offer choice and challenge.* Help students challenge themselves by offering choices that appeal to them—or help them discover the choice. This is not always possible, but choice and challenge lead to better performance and increased respect.

Principle 2: Don't forget the basics.

Coaching has its limitations and will not be effective with all students. Judge your efforts by your sincere attempts to change behaviors or help students perform, not by the need to change every student's behavior. If you feel frustrated, go back to the basics below. It's a simple list, but reflects proven coaching practices that work.

- *Stop thinking of exceptions.* Remember the 80/20 rule: 20% of your students may resist coaching, but 80% will respond. Go with the majority.
- *Know what needs training versus what needs to be communicated.* Train for the more challenging tasks, but for ordinary tasks, expect compliance. Not all actions require coaching help. Use your judgment to decide when to train—and when to instruct.

- *Identify behaviors driving the performance.* Always seek to under-stand the behavior behind the actions. For example, underneath a bored attitude often lies anger. Behind disengagement is family dysfunction and loss of love. Defiance may be aimed at you, but meant for someone else. Use your counseling skills, if you feel confident. If not, consult and get help. Remember that a caring attitude is never a mistake.

Principle 3: Use a six-step protocol.

A protocol enables coaching conversations to go more smoothly. This protocol need not be mechanical—just use it bring consistency to your approach with students. In itself, this model of interaction will teach students how they can interact with their peers and teammates.

- *Ask the student what he or she is doing well.* Always begin with the positive, and work from the perspective of the student. Your initial job is to listen, observe, and gather data.
- *Give positive feedback.* Speak in specific terms and respond as directly as you can to student comments. This is not an opportunity to over praise or indulge students. Simply acknowledge what has gone right.
- *Ask the student to identify what he or she is not doing well.* Work again from the student's perspective. Once you have listened atten-tively and acknowledged success, the door opens to self-reflection. Encourage students to identify specific behaviors that will improve performance.
- *Give observations or data as feedback.* Judgment is not effective, particularly with young people. Provide feedback in the form of obser-vations of fact, not inference. Example: "I see you failed the test," rather than, "Why didn't you study?"
- *Define what a good job looks like.* Be specific about what you want from students. Use videos or exemplars to show students the right method or outcome. Makes sure they know what top performance looks like.
- *Offer training.* What specific help or resources can you offer for students to improve? Let them know where and how to find assistance.

Principle 4: Help students take action.

Coaching is not effective unless you can give students specific feedback or suggestions for improvement. This varies from large, "attitude-adjustment" suggestions to small, discrete steps that students can take to improve perfor-mance. This is the core challenge of coaching, particularly since students all require a slightly different message from a coach. Plus, students may require different challenges and tasks to succeed.

- *Name the behavior to change.* The best approach with a struggling student is to observe, wait, and reflect before offering suggestions for improvement. Release judgments and respond to what you observe rather than what you assume. Give students specific recommendations that distinguish the new behaviors from the old and help students reach a new standard.
- *Differentiate the task.* Adjust the task or role of the student if necessary. Your goal as a coach is to present the student with the right level of challenge.
- *Use "low stakes," formative assessment.* Your goal is to move from a "culture of earning to a culture of learning" (Schwartz, 2014c). Offer lots of formative feedback that has nothing to do with grades. Create a rich culture in which students know that you value personal performance.
- *Project certainty.* There is always a next step for a student. Help him or her identify that next step and believe that the student can do it. In this case, I mean *really* believe. It has to be heartfelt.
- *Let them know you'll be back.* Coaching is not a one-off intervention. Change requires much more than one conversation with a student. Good coaches remain patient and hopeful, but exude certainty.

If this sounds like too much to remember, just go back to basics and practice acceptance. Simple works!

Moving Forward . . .

Overcoming Judgment

The teaching profession operates on judgment. We judge performance, attitude, and mastery of information. We give grades, evaluate, and highlight test scores. In my view, there's nothing wrong with competition, evaluation, or even grades. But another legacy should bother us: the tendency to confuse character with competence.

This is a daily challenge for anyone, in any walk of life. But for a teacher, the challenge is exceptional. For a teacher to hold a duality in their minds (and hearts)—that every child is equally worthy, even if

(Continued)

(Continued)

they express their intelligence in different ways or *refuse* to share—is an act of sainthood. There is a radical difference between wondering, "How intelligent is this kid?" versus thinking, "How is this child intelligent?" (see Markham, 2012). This is the domain of unconditional love and acceptance.

This is a highly personal journey, I realize. The typical educational resource will be of much less service to you than meditation or reflection on your values and beliefs. So I will suggest two very practical steps:

1. ***Don't participate in the usual staffroom discussions about student failure or deficiencies****.* Have you noticed the tenor of conversations that teachers have about students can often be relentlessly negative? An understandable weariness has crept into the teaching profession, though I have every hope that focusing on deep intelligent behaviors will revive and invigorate teaching (and that is the case already, for schools that make skills and habits of mind central). Just don't participate or add to the negativity.

2. ***Don't apologize for your focus on care and positivity.*** OK, not the usual prescription. But now you've read some of the latest science on positive psychology, the heart–brain connection, and evidence that people in close proximity are trading a lot more information that we previously believed. I once read a note on my staff room bulletin board regarding a co-worker's sickness. "Send good thoughts," it said. Why not? Radiate your belief that unconditional acceptance helps every child be more intelligent. Remember how thoughts connect. Your positive thinking may have an impact on your colleagues!

Reflection Questions . . .

1. Do you unconsciously judge students by appearance or demeanor?

2. What is your success rate with "difficult" students?

3. Will the pressure to cover your curriculum keep you from being a good coach? If so, are there solutions?

8 Put Thinking First

Teacher as Designer

Let's take a brief walk through history. The received model of learning took root in the citadels of the 1500s, where theologians-turned-professors dispensed knowledge to acolytes and students. Their knowledge came from "on high"; nearer to God meant well informed and better educated. Their goal was to share the catechism through information transfer, with acolytes faithfully receiving and recording the thoughts of their teachers in books. To "read" the books afterwards, as reading was originally defined, was to engage in a deliberative process that valued showing fidelity to the ideas that had been accumulated.

Since then, science has taken its long march to define learning as a cognitively oriented, brain-based process that rewarded logic and belittled emotions, a viewpoint strongly reinforced by the input–output metaphor of the computer age. That view is strongly supported by our current image of "brainpower," which conjures up a picture of complex wiring and multiple circuits employed to circulate massive numbers of signals through the cortex. Clusters of cortical neurons go to work on a task, amplifying the signals through release of neurotransmitters until the appropriate region of the brain lights up. Magically, it seems, at the same moment a student might solve a difficult calculus problem. Learning has occurred; thinking has happened.

At least we assume so. Do the neurons really light up? No, not really. Those wonderful color photos of a brain at work are ghost images, not actual shots of thoughts. Brain scans use the magnetic properties of blood that is flowing to that region of the brain to create the images. The presence of blood means the brain must be using those neurons to think.

That's the theory, and it's not unreasonable. But the explanatory gap between a simple physiological surge of blood and solving complex problems or appreciating Shakespeare should give us pause. I would urge the attitude of the successful Google employee: Let's have some humility and admit that thinking is utterly mysterious. Bit by bit, we're dissecting the brain. But we're not one step closer to understanding thinking.

I'm going to make the radical suggestion that thinking, whatever the process, involves more than the brain. The research into the brain, heart, and emotions tells us that the brain is a dynamic organ wired into the entire body and tuned to the surrounding ecosystem, making it imperative that our notion of good thinking and where it comes from be expanded and nourished.

LETTING GO OF THE OLD MENTAL MODEL: FIVE DESIGN PRINCIPLES

The end result of over 500 years of "thinking about thinking" is that the received model is alive and well, and has become a deeply embedded mental model of learning as modular. Think, for example, of metaphors used every day in classrooms: *It went in one ear and out the other;* she didn't *get it* or couldn't *grasp it;* or our desire to *build* knowledge in students by stacking units in the right sequence.

I propose that this embedded model, now hardwired into the teaching DNA, presents a difficult challenge for teachers. By implementing new inquiry-based standards, education hopes to promote better thinking through emphasizing problem solving and innovation. Teachers take this mandate seriously. Most teachers create opportunities for thinking, give students feedback on the process, and use open-ended, reflective questions to frame the learning. They make efforts to help students engage in critical thinking, presumably the highest or deepest form of thinking, depending on which metaphors are used.

Teachers are also well aware that information transfer alone will not suffice. As Grant Wiggins (2014b) states at the end of a series of articles on lectures, "It can be said flatly that the mere act of listening to wise statements and sound advice does little for anyone. In the process of learning, the learner's dynamic cooperation is required." Part of that cooperation, as teachers know, involves students getting better at *thinking* for themselves, with teachers acting as mentors and guides.

That's the direction. Inevitably, the world will transition to a thinking system as opposed to a content delivery system, in which fewer standards will be balanced with far more opportunity for design, problem solving, creativity, and interconnected sharing of ideas. Of course, reality intrudes. The knowledge explosion, along with technology, has not been entirely kind to teachers interested in more thinking. Too much information has been translated into too many standards, with too much verbiage attached. That has disrupted *thinking.* A singular focus on standards can leave too little time for teaching thinking or for taking long periods in the classroom in which students mull, discuss, and reflect—the staples of thinking.

If you define the thinking problem as modular—that is, subscribe to the old model of standards as foundation for learning and retention as the outcome—I don't see a solution. The way forward is to integrate thinking, learning, and content into a seamless whole by designing an experience that changes a student's openness to learning, as well as leaving key concepts in his or her mind. That's the *teacher as designer* role. The five design principles in this chapter will help you get started.

RECONNECT THINKING AND ATTITUDE

In *Making Thinking Visible,* a terrific book on thinking that I'll refer to again in this chapter, authors Ron Ritchhart, Mark Church, and Karin Morrison (2011) introduce the keys to coaching thinking, as opposed to lecturing *about* thinking. A first step is crucial: see understanding as the purpose of thinking, not the primary building block.

This is a switch, but it mirrors the development of the holistic skills that more accurately describe how people figure things out in life. A switch in per-spective is involved because most teachers have been raised on the mother's milk of Bloom's Taxonomy, which offers a convenient view of thinking as a hierarchical, building-block exercise. In Bloom's view, good thinking started with remembering and acquiring a knowledge base, then proceeded through applying, analyzing, and evaluating. In the 1990s, creating was added as the culminating higher-order activity.

Beyond the fact that the taxonomy was theoretical and not research based, as is the case with so much of what education takes as gospel (think mul-tiple intelligences or the right/left brain split), the building block approach just doesn't hold up to scrutiny. It misjudges the complexity of thought that results in true understanding, which emerges from a deep, active, constructive internal process spurred by challenge and honed through observation, detecting patterns, and making interpretations.

Unfortunately, the taxonomy at this point may do more harm than good. It has focused teachers on completing work assignments (getting the know-ledge base) and the "tell and practice" routine of many classrooms (apply and analyze). Most damaging, it encourages surface learning—the memori-zation of knowledge and rote facts—rather than deep learning. This won't do in an inquiry system. As Ritchhart and coauthors (2011) put it, "Retention of information through rote practice isn't learning; it is training" (p. 9).

They make the equally valid point that the antidote to rote learning—an activity-based classroom—may not lead to understanding either. Often, activities are simply a more "palatable" way to practice. The goal for inquiry-based coaches needs to be elevated. Rather than thinking about what students need to do to complete an assignment, the focus shifts to examining the authentic intellectual activity at work in the process. Once it becomes explicit, it can be coached.

Seeing attitudes such as openness, persistence, empathy, and flexibility as the key constituents of critical thinking is the exact approach necessary to coach good thinking and inquiry. It allows the inquiry-based teacher to start with *first things first*—the foundation of attitudes that lead to unbiased, flexible approaches to problem solving. There are other skills involved, to be sure. Thinking strategies and knowledge are also prerequisites. But ultimately, critical thinking is not a skill so much as a way of being.

Rethinking Thinking

If behavior and attitude interact with thinking, what does good thinking look like? Roland Case and LeRoi Daniels of the Critical Thinking Consortium at the University of British Columbia have pointed out the disappointing state of critical thinking in schools, mainly the result of the inherent conflict between teaching content and taking the time to get students to think for themselves, but also because of old conceptions that create false divisions between thinking, knowledge, and attitude.

Their first goal—the goal for inquiry-based teaching in general—is to overcome the divisions by recognizing that "thinking without content is vacuous and content acquired without thought is mindless and inert" (Case & Daniels, n.d., p. 2). But their chief contribution to critical thinking, in my view, is that their approach takes critical thinking out of the category as a discrete mental activity separate from other forms of thinking, or as a mental exercise separate from creativity. They emphasize qualities of thinking, not types of operations. More important, they include attitudes as the key constituent of critical thinking, along with four other qualities of thinking that describe critical thinking:

Attitudes or habits of mind

Thinking strategies

Background knowledge

Conceptual knowledge

Criteria for judgment

This view fits well with the recent literature on grit and persistence, the qualities or habits of mind that lead more successful problem solving (Tough, 2012). Good thinking lies near the intersection of deep assets such as motivation, learned optimism, self-control, and character. For example, the list of attributes for an exemplary critical thinker, as offered by Case and Daniels, is really a "360" view of a student's thinking process:

Typical Attributes of Exemplary Critical Thinkers

I.
- are open to new ideas
- persist/have staying power in thinking through a problem
- have empathy/can appreciate others' viewpoints
- have courage of convictions/not afraid to take an unpopular stand
- question ideas/don't accept everything at face value
- don't jump to conclusions/not hasty or rash in coming to a conclusion
- are flexible/willing to change tactics
- don't take themselves too serious/can laugh at themselves
- are willing to live with ambiguity/don't need black-or-white answers
- welcome challenges

II.
- restate a problem in unambiguous language or in graphic form
- confirm understanding by restating in own words
- ask questions which probe for more information
- examine issues from varying perspectives
- look for connections with known features
- test ideas using a "reality check"
- focus on one thing at a time/ break complex challenges into manageable bits
- consider the assumptions presupposed by a position
- look for possible counter-arguments or negative consequences

III.
- have extensive general knowledge/are experienced/are well read
- are knowledgeable about the specific topic

IV.
- recognize common informal fallacies (e.g., straw person/slippery slope)

V.
- recognize good (well supported) arguments
- value clarity and specificity

Source: Case & Daniels, n.d., pp. 3–4.

This list brings us back to the thrive-and-drive ecosystem. With guidance, thinking can get better. But a critical point is that the research into the brain, emotions, and intelligence confirms that thinking involves more than cortical maneuvering. In itself, thinking is a deep bodily process driven by relationships, care, and intelligent behaviors that promote curiosity, awareness, and flexibility. The brain—and therefore thinking—functions as part of the ecosystem. You are part of that ecosystem.

MAKE THINKING COACHABLE

So, as knowledge transfer diminishes and the importance of good thinking becomes more prominent, how do teachers become better coaches of the process? As the authors of *Making Thinking Visible* show, identifying habits of mind and thinking dispositions is a first step to getting inside the black box of the brain and figuring out thinking. This "naming and noticing" includes ways to identify thinking and draw attention to it. When it comes to the brain and thinking, anything we name is an approximation. However, we need models, and the authors begin with guidelines that help reframe thinking as a holistic process visible to an observer.

This is critical to a coach. You can't coach what you can't see. A sports coach can watch athletes in motion, spot techniques, notice flaws, and look at the whole scene again in slow motion video. Coaching inquiry is not so easy. How can you make thinking visible so you can comment, correct, and praise?

Using newer maps of thinking to identify holistic habits of mind required to understand new ideas or evaluate solutions is extremely useful. The maps invite a deeper view of thinking as a whole-body exercise, in which judgment and emotions, and perhaps even intuition, combine to help a student move from a dualistic view of problems (every problem has a right or wrong answer), to multiplicity (some issues involve competing, and often conflicting, points of view), and finally to relativism (thinking "evaluatively" or reflectively to decide relative merits of competing course of action) (Pruett, 2014).

On the surface, these maps don't sound very different from older cognitive schemes for thinking. For example, the authors of *Making Thinking Visible* suggest the following eight kinds of thinking:

1. Observing closely and describing what's there

2. Building explanations and interpretations

3. Reasoning with evidence

4. Making connections

5. Considered different viewpoints and perspectives

6. Capturing the heart and forming conclusions

7. Wondering and asking questions

8. Uncovering complexity and going below the surface of things (Ritchhart et al., 2011)

One legacy of Bloom's Taxonomy is that teachers have been encouraged to focus on understanding rather than application, analysis, synthesis, and evaluation. Instead, the authors suggest a more flexible, open-ended format that models a teacher's interest in the ideas being explored, helps a student construct understanding, and facilitates the illumination of students' own thinking to themselves. As Ritchhart and colleagues (2011) state,

> Each of these represents not so much question types—though they may be classified this way—as they represent goals we have as teachers: to model intellectual engagement, to support students in constructing understanding, and to help students clarify their own thinking. In contrast, a lot of the questions asked in classrooms are about testing students' memory of what was taught. Such questions do not engage learners with ideas; they merely review content. (p. 31)

Two other suggestions round out the picture: listening and documentation. Good questions that drive learning don't arise out of the ethers; they come through interaction and response to student contributions. Good listening captures thoughts and conveys respect, further opening up students to deeper thinking. And when the result of thinking is recorded and documented, it captures the artifacts and discussions or reflections around those artifacts, in effect extending the process of listening and respectful examination.

Using this approach as a foundation, the authors introduce 21 visible thinking routines divided into introducing and exploring ideas, synthesizing and organizing idea, and digging deeper into ideas. These are specific, protocol-based activities that require students to express, share, and evaluate thinking. Each activity can be taught; each makes it possible to coach students for improvement.

I want to note especially that the thinking routines fill the gap perfectly between cognition and redefining smart. It sounds obvious, but thinking and intelligent behaviors need to be two sides of the same coin.

Recall the 50-year message of *affective* versus *cognitive* domains—an approach that perpetuates a split between brain and body. The thinking routines do the opposite. None will succeed ultimately without students bringing the full resources of intelligence to the process of thinking.

The routines also help us give a proper definition to the term *metacognition*. Metacognition implies that a superior cognitive process takes place that looks down at cognition; in fact, as students become more aware of their thinking, they apply persistence, flexibility, and curiosity to future challenges. Rather than some magical muse, it's the application of intelligent behaviors to the situation at hand and stimulating more thinking that makes the difference. Moreover, teachers can't coach this process without bringing the same intelligent behaviors to bear and modeling ways of effective thinking. This returns us to the theme of Chapter 1: inquiry requires walking the walk as well as talking the talk.

Finally, recruiting students into the process of learning starts with building a culture of engagement and inquiry, but without rigorous methods to coach and assess thinking the culture will fail. Building the culture includes beliefs that students want to work harder and think more deeply, not the reverse. Sustaining the culture requires the seeing the growth mindset at work, from both the teacher and the student perspective. That is why visible thinking becomes a crucial component of inquiry-based education.

START WITH QUESTIONS

If you need guidance or reassurance on how to coach students in science or math, I suggest a list of guiding principles developed by two inquiry-based science teachers, who define their method as *open inquiry,* meaning they start with a general plan but no particular set of instructions for how the unit should go (Bresser & Fargason, 2013). I won't list all 10 principles, only the first one, which sums up nicely the approach to facilitating and stimulating thinking: "You don't have to know everything."

That's a good attitude to elicit good thinking: start with questions. In a traditional classroom, teachers remain the center of attention and owners of knowledge and information. In an inquiry environment, the goal is to help students formulate their own questions. In fact, inquiry flips the roles of teacher and students: students ask, and teachers answer.

Terry Heick, originator of *TeachThought,* a site devoted to inquiry-based learning, puts questioning as one of the four cardinal phases of the inquiry process, emphasizing that teachers should model questioning and use methods such as "thinks aloud" to revise flawed questions, concept mapping tools to analyze thinking, Socratic seminars, and question formulation techniques (QFT) (see www.teachthought.com).

QFT is a technique described in *Make Just One Change: Teach Students to Ask Their Own Questions,* by authors Dan Rothstein and Luz Santana (2011), who flip the Socratic Method on its head. Their QFT asks students to come up with questions that speak to the core of the topic. The quest is for the question, not the answer. Often the process takes place in groups, with four rules to encourage an "opening up" of the process: (1) Ask as many questions as you can (gives license to ask); (2) do not stop to discuss, judge, or answer any question (creates safe space and protection); (3) write down every question exactly as it is stated (levels the playing field so all questions and voices are respected); and (4) change any statement into a question (insists on the discipline of phrasing, asking, and thinking in questions, not statement).

For coaches, it's important to remember that opening up students to asking questions is a two-step process. Fear of judgment or embarrassment closes down many students, so the connection between student and teacher matters. Staying present, speaking slowly, increasing positivity, speaking warmly, and listening deeply will elicit far better questions than an interrogative manner.

What Is Authentic?

Voice and choice—the opportunity for students to engage in designing their own learning or shaping the learning to their needs—is popular. There's an obvious reason: authentic education is another way of starting with questions. In schools that practice project-based learning (PBL), an authentic challenge lies at the heart of a good project. In the context of PBL, authentic is defined as the reason to learn. Why is this concept or idea important? Why should students and teacher spend time and energy investigating this topic or question? I recommend the following ideas for PBL teachers:

- *Start with a big idea.* The best projects come from ideas generated while driving or singing in the shower. Often, an idea for a project will surface unexpectedly. Think of ways you can tie the project to your standards or units of instruction.
- *Look within a mile of school.* In every community, problems and challenges exist. Most can be found locally, close to school, or at least in your community. Look for social ills, nature centers, contested issues, or any challenge faced by local government or residents.
- *Read the headlines.* Stay alert for national or global issues that tie into your curriculum. Then, plan the project around the issue, rather than a "current events" day to your teaching.

- *Put a "soft focus" on your standards.* Review your standards in light of the meaning and impulse behind them. Why do students learn about this subject or topic? If the answer is, "It's on the test," then don't plan a project around it. But the powerful concepts behind most standards can help you find a big theme for a project.

- *Think discipline, not subject.* A subject implies a set of facts; a discipline encompasses a set of core ideas, processes, and questions centered on a particular area of life. Use the discipline approach to reach into the heart of your subject and extract the important learning that can be a basis for a project.

- *Frame the idea with concepts and generalizations.* Good ideas can always be framed by major concepts, such as *community, work, interdependence, systems, patterns, interaction,* etc. A good project idea also fits easily into enduring understandings or essential themes. For example, a project focused on a community conflict is an example of a generalization about concepts: *Individuals* and *groups* react to issues and events based on their *values* and *worldviews.*

- *Ask students.* Share with students the standards they will need to learn. How do the learning objectives relate to their lives? How can they be incorporated into an authentic project? (Markham, 2012, p. 59)

Teaching Above the Standards

If PBL is not an option for you, or you're faced with a pre-set curricula, large class size, and too many students suffering from learned helplessness—an unfortunate by-product of too much programmed instruction—it may be more challenging for you to bring authenticity into your teaching. But action and progress are always options. Even if constrained by circumstances, you can bring more engagement, authenticity, and better thinking into your classroom. Here's a great list of ways to teach above the standards that integrate ideas in this book and help you make your standards more authentic.

1. *Make the standards fit into student interests.* Start with student interests and then figure out how standards fit into their interests.

2. *Teach students to question.* Offer students time, space, and techniques for asking good questions.

3. *Focus on the skills and language of learning.* This is making thinking visible. Use the visible thinking routines.

4. *Be open to many answers.* Allow students to discover, not just master material.

5. *Have authentic conversations about motivations.* Get at the "why" of school and the "why" behind every lesson.

6. *Emulate effective risk-taking.* Try some of the riskier methods used by successful teachers at your school. Figure out why students seem to do more thinking in certain classes.

7. *Use professional learning communities.* Talk about thinking and standards. Are we, as educators, accomplishing our most important goals?

8. *Share the many success stories.* Resisting standardization is not easy. There's safety and inspiration in numbers (Schwartz, 2014b).

FOCUS ON INQUIRY AND DESIGN PRACTICES

Coaching thinking requires metacognitive skills beyond using thinking routines as activities. Inquiry implies large-scale design projects, innovation, and use of the scientific methods to master complex issues or design challenges. The renewed emphasis on STEM (science, technology, engineering, and mathematics) programs means importing design practices from industry into the school curriculum. The coach becomes project manager, responsible for keeping creative thinking purposeful, on track, and productive. Specific thinking routines help, but the focus shifts to optimizing design solutions.

Unfortunately, too often the conversation about STEM practices devolves into debates over whether all students should learn code in high school or aim for technology careers. These debates overlook a key fact: the engineering and mathematical *practices* that have begun to take root in education represent a deeper learning approach applicable to all subjects. Crafting a prototype, receiving helpful feedback, designing within constraints, and allowing time and opportunity for reflection and improvement represent best practices in learning theory in general. They are really a cross between skillful thinking and intelligent behaviors—and to implement them, coaching is required.

For example, the new Framework for K–12 science education in the United States (to be applied in the Next Generation Science Standards) offers an extremely rich vision of deep thinking by using three interrelated dimensions for teaching and learning. Combined with "cross-cutting" concepts such as patterns, cause and effect, scale, proportion and quantity, systems and system models, flows and cycles, structure and function, and stability and change, the framework cites eight core scientific and engineering practices involved in the design process. Coaching the thinking of students as they move through this process might look like this:

1. Asking questions and defining problems

2. Developing and using models

3. Planning and carrying out investigations

4. Analyzing and interpreting data

5. Using mathematics, information and computer technology, and computational thinking

6. Constructing explanations and designing solutions

7. Engaging in argument from evidence

8. Obtaining, evaluating, and communicating information

Using Math, Science, and Engineering Practices

Coaching students through the design process involves translating these practices into thoughtful questions that require visible evidence of thinking. Questions like the following, for example, can be posed and coached:

What is the design for?

What are the criteria and constraints of a successful solution?

What models will help visualize a possible solution?

What is the "best" solution?

How can the various designs be compared?

How will the design affect the world around us?

These questions fit nicely with the *practices* sections of the new Common Core standards. The practices represent a new kind of standard, not content based, but process based. They have been added not only to science and engineering, but also to the Common Core State Standards for mathematics, which made a significant, but still under-regarded, shift in emphasis: the development of eight math practices that encourage inquiry, coaching, and intelligent behaviors in ways similar to science and engineering.

1. Make sense of problems and persevere in solving them.

2. Reason abstractly and quantitatively.

3. Construct viable arguments and critique the reasoning of others.

4. Model with mathematics.

5. Use appropriate tools strategically.

6. Attend to precision.

7. Look for and make use of structure.

8. Look for and express regularity in repeated reasoning.

Integrating math and science practices into inquiry-based learning requires a leap of faith and the belief that students don't necessarily require direct instruction in subjects traditionally considered tough and challenging. But it's just another mindshift, really. First, contrary to common beliefs about math, it's not the absence of the math "gene" or a unique intellect that drives achievement—it's motivation. Studies by child development experts show that IQ indicates the starting point for math achievement, but the amount of *new* learning in math is the result of beliefs such as, "If I work harder, I can get better in math." Interestingly, students who focus exclusively on grades as the reward for math performance don't show the same improvement (Blue, 2012).

END WITH REFLECTION

Reflection is the most powerful form of thinking. Consistent, in-depth reflection benefits students by increasing understanding, fostering retention, and heightening curiosity. But aside from reflective writing in English class, it's nearly entirely absent from pacing guides and curriculum. There is *no* time for reflection; Unit 5 has been completed on Friday, and Unit 6 must start on Monday.

This is disastrous on every level. There is no opportunity for metacognition or self-examination on the quality of thinking during the project, both of which anchor learning and encourage further curiosity. Nor does it allow time to enjoy the intrinsic reward of deeper learning and accomplishment, fuel the fire of engagement, or teach reflection as a tool for improvement and growth. It is an anti-growth mindset strategy.

Reflection also symbolizes the commitment to an inquiry-based culture, which depends on recurrent efforts to value and promote thinking. Thinking is not a one-off exercise; it is a way of approaching learning and seeking depth. It needs to be part of the daily experience of students. But stopping the train of instruction to allow students to reflect, as a group, shows particular commitment and respect to the entire process.

Reflection can be a simple, straightforward exercise, as compact as having students answer three questions: What did I like? What do I wonder about? What do I suggest? That's a common protocol (see the Afterword for a full list of suggestions) that works. But any exercise that interrupts the traditional pattern of creating a product and getting a grade (the "hand it in, hand it back" culture) will be welcomed by students. Authors of *The Big Think,* for example, suggest using reflection as a central focus of lessons, in which students continually ask *so what?* questions to examine their deep understanding of a topic (What do I know? Why is this important?) and progress on learning skills (How did I learn what I know? Why is this important?) (Loertscher, Koechlin, & Zwaan, 2009).

One final note: teachers reflect as well. As co-learners in the learning process, it's important to model reflective thinking (What did I do well? What can I improve?). A culture of inquiry begins and ends with every participant committed to growth and reflection.

Moving Forward . . .

When Do Your Students Think?

The authors of *Making Thinking Visible* (Ritchhart et al., 2011) offer a valuable exercise to help you identify discrepancies between classroom activities and teaching that is likely to lead to understanding.

Begin by making a list of all the actions and activities with which your students are engaged in the subject you teach (if you are an elementary school teacher, pick a single subject to focus on, such as math, reading, or writing). You might want to brainstorm the list with a couple of colleagues or teammates. Now, working from this list, create three new lists:

1. The actions students in your class spend most of their time doing. What actions account for 75% of what students do in your classroom on a regular basis?

2. The actions most authentic to the discipline, that is, those things that real scientists, writers, artists, and so on actually do as they go about their work

3. The actions you remember doing yourself from a time when you were actively engaged in developing some new understanding of something within the subject area or discipline

To the extent your first list—what students spend the bulk of their time doing—matches the other two lists, your class activity is aligned with understanding. If the three lists seem to be disconnected from one another, students may be more focused on work and activity than understanding. They may be doing more learning *about* the subject than learning to *do* the subject.

Reflection Questions . . .

1. How do you judge or grade critical thinking in your classroom?

2. Are you offering choice and challenge to your students?

3. What methods do you use to encourage deep thinking in your classroom?

9 Follow the Gamers

The Creative Mindset

Seven years ago, I had just finished several months of work with high schools in California, Oregon, Washington, Texas, North Carolina, Arizona, New Mexico, Wisconsin, Iowa, Colorado, Missouri, and three Canadian provinces. I'd also just become a high school parent. Based on both experiences, I'd say that one part of me was buoyant and optimistic—the other part, well, not so much.

I was hopeful because I visited schools that had begun implementing a set of emerging best practices that included project-based learning, the principles of youth development, and the intentional creation of a coherent, personalized school culture that encourages and supports peak performance. They were focused on the future.

But I was concerned because so many other schools remained relics— and one of those schools turned out to be close to home. At the freshmen orientation meeting at my son's new high school, the principal, to his credit, showed *Shift Happens,* a popular YouTube video about skills and jobs in the future, and how schools could help prepare young people for 21st century life.

Bravo! I was enthused. But then a few days later, the Parent–Student Handbook showed up in the mail. The Handbook opened with the daily schedule, rules and behavior codes, the ban on gang colors—and then moved on to the real poetry, the expulsion policy. From the opening page, the document conjured up a vision of rows of desks, more seat time, the repetitive nature of learning, and the unspoken contract between school and learner that says, You behave and we'll give you a diploma.

Seven years later, by the way, with my son three years out of high school, the Handbook still reads the same way. Nothing has changed, except for updated graphics. And the principal—who told me midway through my son's high school career that project-based learning is for "vocational students"— remains in his position.

OVERCOMING CONFORMITY

How would I have changed the Handbook? I'd begin by welcoming students into a community of learners, both students and teachers, who follow norms, not rules. I'd offer a four-year vision that emphasizes the opportunity students have to achieve personal balance, master a 21st century skill set, and become learners who can handle information of any kind, anywhere, at any time.

I'd also emphasize that this school will help them get into college—but that admission to college is just a by-product of good learning, not an end in itself. I'd make it clear that the school's most important goal is to help students discover their purpose in life—to go deep into themselves and come out the other side with insights about who they are and what they want out of life. And I would allocate the first week of school to discuss these ideas and bring students on board.

Instead, Handbook's message was unmistakable: this institution operates through control and sanctions, and values "staying between the lines" behavior rather than creative engagement with learning. My objection is not to rules, but rather to the subtext of limitation and standardization. For me, the Handbook exemplifies how the vast majority of the 10,000 U.S. high schools have yet to grasp how to motivate and engage today's learners in a more forward vision of learning—especially at a historical moment when creativity and thinking outside the lines has become the prized skill.

Why Creativity Challenges Education

This brings us to the elephant in the room: creativity is driven by purposeful behavior—by *engagement* with life and work. Most coaches and human relations professionals in industry know this well. Some call it PQ (the passion quotient) and consider it far more important than IQ (Friedman, 2013). Joe Robinson, author of *Don't Miss Your Life* (2011), calls it an internal quality—*life intelligence*—that allows one to surrender to an experience, step into the brand new, and not hold back. However defined, creativity requires passion and a full-on commitment to a challenge.

On top of that, once engaged, we may not know how to "teach" creativity. Teaching passionate creativity—or even its close cousin, critical thinking—is not remotely similar to teaching the photosynthesis cycle or the causes of World War One. The skills of innovation and creativity can be lumped into a mysterious set of processes used by human beings to make sense of their world, enter a dark tunnel of confusion, and reemerge with a solution in hand. How this process unfolds, no one knows. How we teach the process, we're not quite sure. Even more difficult is assessing the journey through this dark tunnel and evaluating the end product. Think of judging a piece of modern art. It's that subjective.

With educators under increasing pressure from society to produce the next generation of problem solvers and innovators, these are big issues. But I've found that teachers know the answer. Everyone does, in fact. Teaching creativity means that we "go deep" with children rather than providing them with more information. Either we engage students, or we give up on creativity. There's no middle ground.

Can We Bring Back the Passion?

Yong Zhao, University of Oregon Professor and author of *World Class Learners* (2012b), calls this *double-think* (2012a). It's the ability to hold two contradictory opinions, and believe both of them. The term was coined by George Orwell in his novel *1984,* and it's a fine descriptor of believing that creative, purpose-driven behavior can flourish in institutions that rely solely on a standardized curriculum driven by testing.

Nearly all teachers know this because nearly every teacher is experiencing identical problems with students: lack of engagement, a feeling that the system does not challenge them (that's different from being hard, as you'll read), and a powerful sense that education fails to address the inner life of today's youth.

The results are identical across the globe. "Our students don't like to read," one Japanese teacher said to me, a surprising comment given the stereotypes of Japanese schools, "So we must find ways to engage them." That is the common complaint. In Turkey, an English-language high school teacher offered a similar observation about her students. "They do the work, but they don't really care." But, she added quickly, "I know they care about many things, but not what I teach them."

Even more disturbing are recent studies of boredom. Interestingly, there are *five different* kinds of boredom (Kaplan, 2013). Most are familiar to us—a kind of indifferent, relaxing boredom; a slightly unpleasant, wandering boredom; a restless and searching boredom; and "reactant" boredom, the kind that is so annoying that we will do anything to escape it. But the fifth was new: "apathetic" boredom, a kind of deep boredom associated with learned helplessness and depression. That's the way high school students (in Germany, at least, where the study was conducted) felt 36% of the time. Is that a surprise? Walk by classrooms in typical high school and look in the door.

Where does the passion to learn and think deeply—to have *creative engagement* with the world—come from? Personality, interests, and rewards play significant roles, but research into psychological well-being confirms that students, fundamentally, seek meaning and mastery. To excel at more than attaining a high grade, they need a reason to learn and the sense of accomplishment that comes from understanding and applying their learning.

That's why meaningful challenge and public performance have become integral to best practices in project-based learning. Insights and instances of innovative thinking nearly always emerge when projects require students to rise to an engaging challenge and then show what they know to a knowledgeable audience. With challenge and mastery as the focus, thinking is a by-product. It's a path to self-satisfaction, not a chore.

Is Creativity Declining?

What else do we know? Creativity flourishes on the edge of chaos, in free environments not wedded to right and wrong answers. It often is at odds with compliant behavior. And it is not a purely cognitive act; it connects to emotions, relationships, judgments, and inspiration (Schwartz, 2014e). That is, it is highly dependent on intelligent behaviors. And, given that human performance is not directly teachable, it means setting the conditions under which creativity flourishes. It also means, as in the case of the modern art example, that we may not know creativity until we see it. None of these methods fits well with a data-driven, standards-based accountability system.

The conflicts result in the double-think: we value creativity, but can't teach it. As the authors of *The Creativity Crisis* put it, "The current national strategy for creativity consists of little more than praying for a Greek muse to drop by our houses" (Bronson & Merryman, 2010). It's a strategy that isn't working. Since 1990, about the time standards became popular, creativity began to decline significantly, at least as measured by the Torrance Creativity Index, a standardized set of questions that measures the combination of divergent and convergent thinking that leads to the production of something useful (a pretty standard definition of creativity).

The Torrance test was first administered in 1958, and until 25 years ago creativity had been on the rise. Then it reversed. Remember back to Chapter 3? IQ is going up, but creativity is going down. Not good, especially since an analysis of the Torrance data showed that the correlation to lifetime creative accomplishment was over three times stronger for childhood creativity than childhood IQ.

In an age that demands, rewards, and honors innovation—and at a scientific threshold telling us that the brain responds to novelty with physical changes that increase divergent capacity—the decline in creativity is not merely a dangerous trend. Without intentionally focusing on creativity, we run the risk of true neglect, both for individual students and for a planet looking for solutions to big problems.

RESTORING THE MISSING LINK: PURPOSE

One way to focus our efforts is to pay greater attention to human development and the adolescent brain. Consider the latest research by Bill Damon, a Stanford professor, child development expert, and leading researcher into adolescents. In his book, *The Path to Purpose* (2008), Damon notes that 25% of teenagers claim to have no purpose in life. And, while others "dabble or dream," only 20% have a solid sense of direction.

We don't know if these statistics are high or low since no one has surveyed youth purpose before. But a mountain of data on youth development, adolescent mental health, and developmental psychology suggests that we should care about the findings. Purpose is a critical asset for healthy adulthood. Without a reason to get out of bed in the morning, a host of problems start to show up in people's lives that impact their health, behavior, and productivity.

Purpose also relates directly to the pursuit of new skills and knowledge. Purpose, meaning, and mastery move in tandem (Benard, 2004). Without tapping into a sense of purpose, high schools are reduced to rules and incentives—primarily the promise of college—rather than relying on the deeper wellsprings of learning that lead to the highest levels of student performance.

A surprising number of parents, including the majority in high-achieving suburban high school districts, support this Faustian pact at the moment. The chance at a name-plate university outweighs twinges about too much emphasis on grades and test scores. We've talked ourselves into the notion that schools don't need to produce healthy adults, just people who can get a degree. (That sounds cynical, but our system *is* disease-prone: 60% of high school students show high levels of stress and anxiety.)

There's also too little attention paid to depth. On one of my summer trips, I met a teacher who quit his job because 26 of the 40 high school staff were football coaches, all hired for their coaching prowess and then randomly assigned to teach English, math, and science. Do you think students went deep in those classes, or just on the football field?

Engaging the Adolescent Brain

Research into the brain confirms our intuition about the untapped power of purpose. Dan Siegel, author of *Brainstorm* (2013), cites four qualities of mind unique to teens: (1) *novelty seeking,* which emerges from an increased drive for rewards in the circuits of the adolescent brain that create the inner motivation to try something new and feel life more fully; (2) *social engagement,* which enhance peer connectedness and lead to supportive relationships; (3) *increased emotional intensity,* which gives enhanced vitality to life and a sense of vital drive; and (4) *creative exploration,* which allows new conceptual thinking and an approach to problems with "out of the box" strategies, and the creation of new ideas.

Siegel (2013) says that each of these qualities has an upside and a downside (the reason that teenagers make you both laugh and cry). But the risks diminish and the positive attributes are enhanced in the presence of purpose and meaning. When adults take care to help young people find creative outlets and meaningful challenge, we get healthier adults. As Siegel writes in the introduction to the book:

> While the adolescent years may be challenging, the changes in the brain that help support the unique emergence of the adolescent mind can create qualities in us that help not only during our adolescent years, if used wisely, but also as we enter adulthood and live fully as an adult. How we navigate the adolescent years has a direct impact on how we'll live the rest of our lives. Those creative qualities also can help our larger world, offering new insights and innovations that naturally emerge from the push back against the status quo and from the energy of the teen years. (p. 3)

So I'll drive the point home again: without purpose, it will be nearly impossible to teach creativity and the other so-called "soft" skills identified with success in today's world. The ability to work with a team, become an entrepreneur, or thrive in the face of adversity all derive ultimately from a sense of purpose. For example, adults with a strong sense of purpose show higher levels of empathy, a crucial habit of mind necessary for effective teamwork. Purpose is linked to creativity and innovative problem solving—key goals of millennial education.

Bill Damon suggests that it's not that difficult to help young people develop a sense of purpose. In addition to lessons that connect school to future life activities or larger world issues, he suggests engaging in regular conversations with students about their hopes, dreams, and aspirations in life, as well as recognizing accomplishments that indicate beyond-the-self concerns. This can trigger awareness, since students themselves may fail to see their accomplishments and dreams. I recall asking a 16-year-old boy about his successes in life, to which he replied, "None." Then I probed a bit. It turns out he had recently earned an Eagle Scout designation. Just talking about it changed his posture and the brightness level in his eyes.

But to give up a content-based curriculum, with its deep traditions, proven techniques for controlling behavior and outcomes, and dominating, standardized regimen, is the difficult step. It feels like giving a 14-year-old the keys to the car and a full tank of gas. It's scary. But if adults are serious about meeting their responsibilities to prepare students to enter the world of the 21st century, it will not be accomplished by adhering to an obsolete model of academic learning that teaches skills as widgets—or by repeating outdated rules. I like the quote attributed to Albert Einstein: "We can't solve problems by using the same kind of thinking we used when we created them." Instead, schools must create a system of learning that melds the noble aspirations of education to the new technologies of personal success. It is the key to supporting young people's desire for purposeful achievement, social engagement, and mastery of essential skills.

That's why I believe that the shift into the next, non-industrial phase of schooling is a psychological issue, not just a logistical one. Fortunately, humans are inherently creative and seem to invent just-in-time solutions to complex challenges. Just when we need a new model of learning that relies on purpose and engagement for success, one has been created, inadvertently, through play.

SHIFTING TO A GAMING MENTALITY

The strategies to motivate students in school have been well identified—and well researched. For example, learning columnist and author of The Brilliant Blog Annie Murphy Paul (2013) lists six research-based strategies as keys to more engagement: (1) Fine-tune the challenge by asking students to work at the very edge of their abilities; (2) start with the question, not the answer; (3) encourage students to beat their personal best; (4) connect abstract learning to concrete situations; (5) make it social; and (6) go deep.

This is a worthy list for increasing motivation. But if we want to liberate the ultimate powers of creativity and critical inquiry, I'd add one more point: *Make it joyful.* In fact, I'm going to circle back to points I made in the early chapters about the positive emotions and the heart. To my mind, it's clear that creativity and the emotion of joy are reciprocal processes. The feeling of challenge, discovery, and mastery resonates through the processes of the heart and instantly flood the brain with impulses that activate the frontal lobes, the part of the brain responsible for insight and creativity.

Most of us know this, or have experienced it. It's the basis for the well-known "flow state," the experience of intense pleasure and effortless concentration on an engaging challenge (Csikszentmihalyi, 1990). Creativity, critical inquiry, and innovation are natural outcomes of deep inquiry. But joy adds the secret ingredient to the sauce. If you can design learning so that students experience joy, the magic starts. Engagement is a non-issue, or a kind of funny one.

Adding *Fiero* to Your Teaching

Joy is not generally associated with the 8 am to 3 pm schedule of a student. But after 3 pm? That can be a different story, and a substantial portion of the population, adults or 14-year-olds, knows why: the entire list of strategies that engage learners, plus the joy, is a perfect description of *what the gamers do*. In fact, gamers now wrap the list into a new word: *fiero*. Fiero is the rush of excitement that gamers experience when they overcome challenges and discover creative solutions that advance their progress in a game.

What do we know about fiero? Jane McGonigal, who wrote *Reality Is Broken* (2012), a book about bringing gaming into the real world, describes it this way:

> Fiero, according to researchers at the Center for Interdsiciplinary Brain Science Research at Stanford, is the emotion that first created the desire to leave the cave and conquer the world. It's a craving for challenges that we can overcome, battles we can win, and dangers we can vanquish.
>
> Scientists have recently documented that fiero is one of the most powerful neurochemical highs we can experience. It involves three different structures of the reward circuitry of the brain, including the mesocorticolimbic center, which is most typically asscosciated with reward and addiction. Fiero is a rush unlike any other rush, and the more challenging the obstacle we overcome, the more intense the fiero. (p. 33)

Why that word? The Italian word *fiero* comes from the same Latin root as *fierce* and is related to *feral*, invoking a feeling of wildness, empowerment, and playfulness, in which constraints, inhibitions, and self-consciousness fall away. What better words do we have to describe the creative process?

Gamification is the Next Big Thing in learning, but not only because it taps deep wellsprings of creativity and purpose. In 2013, the American Psychological Association published a study that identified some of the benefits of gaming, including "'faster and more accurate attention allocation, higher spatial resolution in visual processing, and enhanced mental rotation abilities'" (in Shapiro, 2014).

This is the strict cognitive view—the human as wired machine—but evidence points to gains in metacognition and intelligence as well. Video games nurture the growth mindset by offering gamers the opportunity to overcome obstacles and rise to challenge by probing their performance, addressing their weaknesses, and adjusting their approach accordingly. Contrary to popular notion, games are quite social as well, with over 70% of gamers playing games with other people. In essence, games teach critical thinking, problem solving, innovation, perseverance, and interpersonal skills—a very nice definition of lifelong learning.

How can your curriculum mirror the attributes of games? I'll take a list created by James Gee (2011), Professor of Literacy Studies at Arizona State University and author of *What Video Games Have to Teach Us About Learning and Literacy* (2003), and turn it into a to-do list:

1. *Focus on well-ordered problems, not facts and information.*

2. *Give students good tools to solve problems.*

3. *Offer goals, but encourage students to rethink goals.*

4. *Lower the cost of failure.*

5. *Put performance before competence and encourage learning by doing.*

6. *Give copious feedback.*

7. *Connect learning to social interaction and mentoring though collaborative play.*

8. *Continually challenge students.*

9. *Use stories to create engagement.*

10. *Hold everyone to same standards, but allow for different pace and mastery.*

CREATIVE EXPRESSION: TEACH OR INSPIRE?

The disconnect between a culture of innovation and a culture of schooling endures for now. But it *will* end. Innovative schools (see the Afterword), inspired teachers, and a generation of students who refuse school as tedium will act as a combined force to shift schools in the direction of inquiry, creativity, and collaborative productivity.

The inquiry system itself spurs creativity and innovation. Honoring the inner life, starting with strengths, focusing on deeper learning, and coaching students to think and reflect constitute a set of best practices for helping students find and express their roots of inspiration.

But possessing a smaller, more routine set of skills that foster creativity and innovation contributes even more to the process. Assuming that students want to be creative and adjusting you daily conversations and interactions with students to support creativity is the key. Over time, it infuses the class-room with a creative energy that builds upon itself. For you, engagement will not be the problem.

What else will work for you? Try these:

1. Orient to potential.

A question we should ask ourselves (and a question on the minds of researchers, no doubt) is this: Does the growth mindset indicate potential leaps in creativity? If IQ, a quality formerly thought to be hardwired into the brain, can increase, why not *openness to experience,* a broad personality trait made up of a varied mix of inquisitiveness, creativity, adventuresomeness, and intelligence (Hiam, 2011)? This is no small matter for educators, if you recall Chapter 4. According to the research of John Hattie (2009), openness is the key factor to productive learning in general.

Statistically, we're not doing well as educators in this category. One expert on creativity in the classroom offers these numbers: Ask a group of second-graders, "Do you think you're creative?" and about 95% of them will answer, "Yes." Three years later, when the kids are in fifth grade, that propor-tion will drop by 50%. And by the time they are seniors in high school? 5% (Lehrer, 2012)!

A good first step, I believe, is to orient to potential and never to problems. The fact is, we don't know much about creativity. But most of us possess hidden reserves of playfulness, wonder, and a desire to make or experience change in life. Assuming that students have the same hidden store of inspi-ration honors that potential and encourages its expression. *Attitude equal altitude* is an old saying. It works.

What attitudes should we seek to encourage? Inventive behavior thrives among people who exhibit self-efficacy (the feeling of control, mastery, and making a difference), intrinsic behaviors (they don't need the grade, but like the learning for its own sake), and enjoy trial and error experimentation (they aren't daunted or discouraged by failure).

The last quality—the willingness to fail—is critical. Tony Wagner of Harvard School of Education and author of *Creating Innovators* (2012b) names learning to take risks and learn from mistakes as one of the five keys to supporting innovative growth in the classroom. That's another iteration of "grit"—the ability to persevere through challenges and frustrations. And how important is using trial and error versus the risk avoidance common in schools? Wagner mentions that at IDEO, a world famous design firm consistently recognized as one of the most innovative companies in the world, the motto is, "Fail early and often" (Wagner, 2012a).

2. Speak the language of creativity.

A teacher's attitude can spur creativity or squelch it. Let's go back to the research. Student performance is affected by self-fulfilling belief systems *and* by teacher beliefs. Students who move from a fixed mindset to a growth mindset will believe in themselves, and in their creative potential. Yet in every school I visit, I hear teachers talking about who is "smart" or "gifted" or a "slow" learner. Aside from the placebo effect this conversation induces, it violates what we know about the brain: the brain is a plastic organ capable of change over a lifetime—and is particularly shifting between ages 5 and 18. Sorting students by assuming who has potential and who doesn't kills the creative urge, not to mention the damage it does to Algebra I scores ("I can't do math—I didn't get the math gene").

3. Design work that matters.

Attitude won't matter much if students complete too many worksheets or see homework as meaningless tasks, or if school remains disconnected from student interests. Inquiry is a personalized system, so that works well. But the supreme challenge in a standards-based system backed by high-stakes assessments that rewards convergent thinking is to fuel creativity in the classroom with its opposite: *divergent* thinking.

Another strange fact: as children, our divergence capability operates at a genius level, but by adulthood the ability to think divergently decreases dramatically (Goodman, 2014). Obviously, this is a valid shift—we can't be immersed in imaginative play at all times. But the ability to enter into that imaginative realm at will is important these days, so encouraging that mental and emotional flexibility (an intelligent behavior) should be part of the teaching plan.

That means applying algebra to the real world, leaving time for exploration in science, or—at every opportunity possible—allowing students to enter a constructivist mode. To *create rather than consume* is another bullet on Tony Wagner's (2012a) list. In an innovative culture, students should acquire knowledge on an as-needed basis, as a means to an end, not to fulfill testing requirements. And, counterintuitively: if they apply information in a meaningful context, they perform quite well on tests and actually retain the information.

4. Be innovative yourself.

Charles Leadbeater, the British futurist and educational innovator, has good insights into creativity. In *Learning From the Extremes,* a recent report for Cisco Systems, Leadbeater and Wong (2010) recommend that schools start "learning from challenges that people face rather than from a formal curriculum" (p. iv). Teachers can either "cover" standards, or turn them into concepts and problems to be solved. Inquiry works towards supporting the kind of "out of the box" thinking we need for the future.

This is the kicker, because innovation requires the willingness to fail, a focus on fuzzy outcomes rather than standardized measures, and the bravery to resist the system's emphasis on strict accountability. But the reward is a kind of liberating creativity that makes teaching exciting and fun, engages students, and—most critical—helps students find the passion and resources necessary to design a better life for themselves and others.

When in doubt, keep in view the overriding challenge is now coming to the fore in public consciousness: we need to reinvent just about everything. Whether scientific advances, technology breakthroughs, new political and economic structures, environmental solutions, or an updated code of ethics for 21st century life, everything is in flux—and everything demands innovative, out of the box thinking. So it follows that education should focus on fostering innovation by putting curiosity, critical thinking, deep understanding, the rules and tools of inquiry, and creative brainstorming at the center of the curriculum.

5. Tap into your student's creative confidence.

Inspiration, purpose, and creativity come through reflection and intention. Having students craft a personal mission statement that defines who they want to be and their purpose in life is a great exercise for liberating and encouraging creativity. Use the diagram in Figure 9.1 as a guide.

Figure 9.1 Crafting a Personal Mission Statement

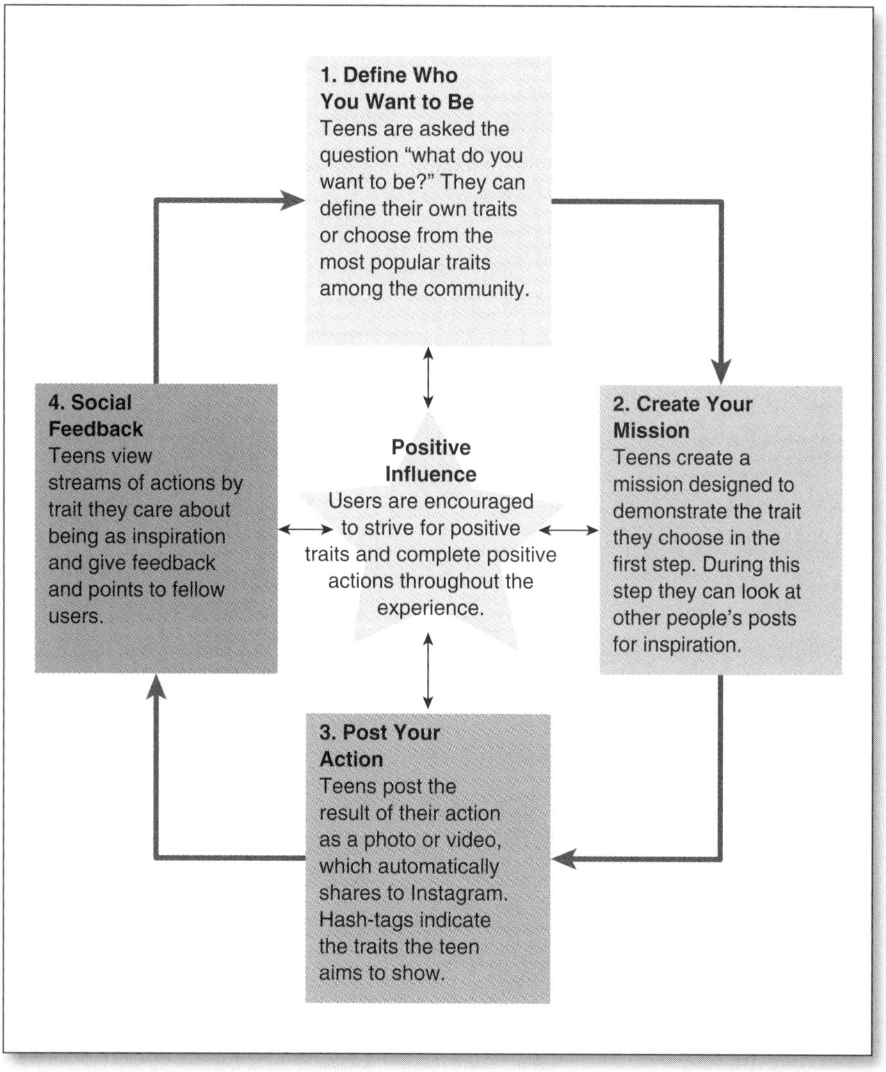

1. Define Who You Want to Be
Teens are asked the question "what do you want to be?" They can define their own traits or choose from the most popular traits among the community.

4. Social Feedback
Teens view streams of actions by trait they care about being as inspiration and give feedback and points to fellow users.

Positive Influence
Users are encouraged to strive for positive traits and complete positive actions throughout the experience.

2. Create Your Mission
Teens create a mission designed to demonstrate the trait they choose in the first step. During this step they can look at other people's posts for inspiration.

3. Post Your Action
Teens post the result of their action as a photo or video, which automatically shares to Instagram. Hash-tags indicate the traits the teen aims to show.

Source: OpenIDEO, Brad Filice.

Moving Forward . . .

Beyond the "A"

Receiving an A in a class doesn't really reward innovation or satisfy the urge for creativity. In fact, in standardized systems of learning there is

(Continued)

(Continued)

no good way to reward breakthrough thinking. One solution is to use rubrics with a "breakthrough" category—a blank column that invites students to deliver a product that cannot be anticipated or easily defined in words. It's not the A category—that's Mastery or Commended or a similar high-ranking indicator. The breakthrough column goes beyond the A, rewarding innovation, creativity, and something new outside the formal curriculum. It's a "show me" category.

Students like it, and so do teachers. It particularly appeals to high-end students who feel current offerings are drab, or to the middling student who will not work just for a grade, but who seeks the psychic reward of creating something cool. To obtain samples of these rubrics, see the Afterword and links to resources.

You might also try the badge system. Digital badges work much like scout badges—they are a symbol of an accomplishment, skill, quality, or interest. They set can be used to set goals, motivate behaviors, represent achievements, or communicate success. They're an excellent tool for capturing the benefits of informal learning or to recognize creative breakthroughs. Most important, badges emerged from games. To students, they will feel current, creative, and exciting.

Reflection Questions . . .

1. What is creativity to you? Do you consider yourself to be creative? Why or why not?

2. Do you think that people are born with creativity, or do they learn it?

3. How would you distinguish creativity from innovation?

10 Tap the Future of Smart

Making Collaboration the Norm

Recently, a seventh-grade teacher told me a story that thrilled her. She had passed a team of four students in the quad at lunchtime and overheard them having a spirited debate about what they had learned in their latest project in her class. They were exchanging cogent ideas, using the vocabulary of the discipline, and listening carefully to each other's arguments. That was all the evidence she needed to know that her project had met its goals. They weren't just socializing; they were *talking*.

But a deeper process was at work, one invisible to the eye. Using our knowledge of brain plasticity, we know that in the presence of attention and purposeful engagement, the brain is working very hard. Thousands of synapses every second are formed and reformed. The interaction between brains promotes a high level of engagement with each other, requires the intentional use of appropriate terms and vocabulary, and challenges inattention and mediocrity.

It's a bidirectional process as well. A two-way interaction between the group and the individual takes place. Individuals shift the intelligence of the group as a whole; at the same time, the individual begins to reflect the influences of the group. How this happens is not a mystery, either. Research into the heart and positive emotions shows how—and why—learning is social in nature (Murphy Paul, 2012). That research extends our prior understanding that groups working in harmony and with a shared purpose experience emotional safety and care—a culture of warmth and trust, not competition and exclusion—that spurs creative thinking and shifts the brain into a peak state. Once in this state, cooperative behaviors have been shown to be contagious, with a kind of cascade effect that promotes kindness, happiness, and generosity (Dossey, 2010).

THE FUTURE OF SMART

Now move to our emerging world. Our brains, which once functioned in relative isolation, are now networked to seven billion other brains. The term *global brain,* often used to describe this phenomenon, is associated with the wired and cloud-based technologies that form the backbone for the on-demand life, especially the daily impact of the billions of bits of accumulated metadata that bathe us, help track our whereabouts, and now constitute a new library of information that will be forever available.

That's not an exaggeration. In 2006, the Library of Congress in the United States began to archive all tweets from Twitter accounts. Every tweet, blog comment, and review across the planet is indexed into someone's search engine. (Lest you think that's a lot of worthless information to catalog, education is the number one industry that uses Twitter. Hopefully, educators elevate the dialogue.)

The interconnected nature of today's world means inevitably that intelligence is a social phenomenon. For purposes of research, it's often referred to as *distributed* intelligence, the study of how the individual human mind is expanding through increasing visual communication, social creativity, instant communication, and collaborative contributions (Fischer, 2006). The resulting increase in human intellectual capability results in what Clay Shirky, author of *Cognitive Surplus* (2010), calls a historic opportunity to use our new collective resource for positive change and innovation.

For now, most of us wonder where all this data sharing will lead, and how a constant stream of information will affect thinking, cognition, memory, and so forth. But given findings on neuroplasticity, it's inevitable that the interaction between hyperconnectivity, metadata, and the human mind will affect intelligence. Whether good things or bad things result, we just don't know. We will get smarter together—or not.

That's the long view, but it's not much help to educators, so I propose another line of thinking about education, the global brain, and distributed intelligence: to think of students (and yourself) as operating in a world of increasing collective intelligence, which experts define as groups of individuals acting collectively in ways that seem intelligent (Malone, 2012).

That's a good working definition for teachers. Young people themselves will define the new parameters for intelligence. Along with your students, you're involved in a kind of action research project to figure out the future. Of course, this may take a generation or two. In the meanwhile, your goal is to develop the mechanisms, protocols, opportunities for meaningful collaboration, and train students in essential people skills to support the new paradigm. At a minimum, this means no more "group" work. It's time to move to an intentional model of collaboration in the classroom.

INQUIRY AND THE CONNECTED WORLD

Before moving to practical steps for forming and assessing teams and collaboration, I want to speculate on the scientific justification behind the philosophical shift to an inquiry model of learning. I apologize to readers who find science tedious, but here's the fact: science tells us that collaborative inquiry may be the only way that we can teach students to manage and adapt to their complex, chaotic, and ever-shifting world.

It's not a stretch to say that physics and biology point to a more fluid, student-centered, problem-oriented system of learning in the future. Both fields now officially define each of us as an "open system." Infinite bits of information coded into waves sweep through the energetic fields of the brain and body, altering pattern recognition responses, affecting emotional states, and recoding DNA.

How waves interact, resonate, and collapse and create material changes in the body is the subject of *entanglement.* That's a field of study traditionally left to quantum physicists, but it should tell you something that the fastest growing subdiscipline in biology is biophysics. It also may tell us why collective intelligence is on the rise—and how that intelligence may help us.

Overall, an entangled world behaves much differently than previously believed. From Newton forward, the idea of a linear, orderly progression of events—the clockwork universe—sustained science. But new mathematical constants show otherwise. Large scale, seemingly random, systems obey the hidden rules of *chaos* and *complexity.* It may seem arcane and unnecessary, but these are two words that inquiry-based teachers should be familiar with.

Those terms entered the lexicon a short 50 years ago, when Edward Lorenz discovered that weather patterns and other natural systems, rather than operating in random patterns, in fact have within them a hidden order.

Since then, the mathematical principles of chaos and complexity have been found to apply to all dynamic systems, including insect colonies, immune responses, economies, the World Wide Web, human society, gene expression, quantum fields, evolution, and—hopefully, of interest to teachers—the brain and consciousness, (How in the heck do those 100 billion neurons act in unison so a student can make sense of my lesson?)

The rules of chaos and complexity are arcane, but one has become familiar to us: earlier, I used the butterfly and the monsoon analogy, in which a small event on one side of the world—in this case, the flapping of a butterfly's wings—results in major reverberations on the opposite side, such as a major weather event. This tells us that a lone butterfly can do a lot of damage, even with a one-day lifespan. And, with the tools of technology now ubiquitous, it also means that small "inputs" can create large-scale change quickly. Think about the impact of 140 characters from one Twitter message on a crowd.

Are We Adapting?

This may be new for us, but not for other species. Another population with some kind of Twitter system is fire ants. If a six-inch divide in the ground (which to ants resembles the Grand Canyon) suddenly stalls their march, a brigade instantly breaks off from the main pack, bonds itself into an ant bridge, and allows the rest of the troops to continue. Insect biologists refer to the bridge building by these annoying, but quite smart, fire ants, as evidence of *swarm intelligence.*

As you probably guess, each ant is not so bright individually. An ant—or a member of a flock, school, hive, or colony—responds to simple rules and uses relatively tiny brains to demonstrate very intelligent behavior as a whole. Note that the ants don't spend any time arguing before building the bridge. Communication is virtually instant, either though pheromones or shifts in energetic fields. That's a worthy model in a global world—and that's the shift needed in our own thinking if we hope to benefit from collective intelligence.

Using the rules of complexity, swarm intelligence has been applied to routing trucks, scheduling airlines, guiding robots, or choosing the best way to disperse telephone calls over large-scale networks. Swarm dynamics also help predict the spread of forest fires or the growth of species in an environment. Nature teaches us, as usual, and how ants or any other species learn to act swiftly and intelligently as a whole, or evolve such admirable capability, is one topic that complexity addresses. Simply think of complexity this way: birds do it; bees and ants do it; now, with the aid of technology, humans have taken up the habit as well.

Chaos is an unfortunate term that can be traced to the Greek word for "void," making it an excellent candidate for connoting confusion and disorder, and reinforcing the image of the volatile, uncertain, ambiguous environment that's driving everyone crazy. In the western mindset, this translates into anti-order, a kind of synonym for extreme randomness. It fits the personality of cynics perfectly.

The common image, however, hides a secret truth about the world: it's highly organized, just not in the way we once believed. Chaos might be considered as "not-order" if you prefer. In reality, chaotic systems create patterns, use information, and evolve and learn through self-organization, meaning the parts and the whole work together without a central controller to create the famous "the whole is greater than its parts" mantra. If you look closely, that describes the global brain at work. Think of youth and their connected world. Why wouldn't that be the future of intelligence for *their* generation?

SEEING COLLABORATION AS THE CORE COMPETENCY

Most teachers use groups, but feel uneasy or dissatisfied with the intellectual outcomes of group work. I believe the reason behind this is that we as educators are in the early stages of learning how to use collaborative learning to achieve high performance. So we have a gap. In today's world, collaborative groups in schools must step up to meet the requirements of the global age, a process in which teams routinely focus on a problem, design solutions, and navigate differences to achieve a result, with members using a variety of thinking tools to brainstorm and improve their ideas, and relying on evidence, facts, persuasive arguments, and knowledge of the subject to succeed. But we haven't yet built these new skills into team routines in the classroom.

It's not that students are uncomfortable in groups (except when experience tells them that only one member of the group will do any work, and the others will run for cover). Whether it's putting a "Like" on a Facebook post, retweeting an idea, or blogging an opinion and receiving feedback, they've operated in a native environment of networked, collective intelligence since birth.

But school groups are different. Rarely is the norm set for individuals to bring their singular gifts to a communal discussion, assimilate information from multiple sources, and sample each other's ideas before passing judgment or deciding a course of action.

This means that it is vital that educators help students move from a Facebook culture to a *thinking* Facebook culture. The ultimate promise of good teamwork is that young people may learn collective ways to think more deeply about their world and design a better future.

Why Students Get Smarter Together

The question is, What do educators do about all this? Can we make students smarter and are there ways to make teams of students smarter? In the next section, I'm going to suggest one immediate fix: to replace the language of groups with the language of teams in the classroom. The language of teamwork commits students and teachers to greater purpose, cohesion, and accountability. That's a first step to overcoming the traditional focus on the individual scholar, a model less relevant each year to the outside world.

A second step, I suggest, is to see collaboration as the key or fundamental 21st century skill. The four Cs listed previously—collaboration, communication, critical thinking, and creativity—all work fine as a list. But closer inspection reveals that they're not equal. The latter three skills blossom in the presence of rich, interactive environments.

Researchers who focus on emotional intelligence and collaboration in team environments know this phenomenon well (Cox, 2011). Individuals competent in self-awareness, social awareness, and relationship management (the three clusters of emotionally intelligent behaviors) are aware of their weaknesses; view constructive criticism positively; recognize the impact of their emotions on colleagues; understand the importance of trust, equality, and camaraderie; and know how to influence others respectfully. This translates into high-functioning teams that display the enthusiasm, productivity, and organizational effectiveness that leads to greater communication, problem solving, and creativity.

Interestingly, just as the *g* factor is used to identify intelligence in individuals, there is also evidence that groups cohere to the extent that they perform as individuals (Malone, 2012). They are able to "pick things up" more quickly. Studies have identified three factors that correlate most significantly with this group ability: (1) the average social perceptiveness of group members; (2) the evenness of conversational turn-taking; and (3) the percentage of women in the group (which might be the power of the X chromosome or the fact that social perceptiveness correlates with gender—or both!).

All of the above, it nearly goes without saying, work better with adults than 14-year-olds. But if we want to teach problem solving, encourage creativity, and graduate flexible thinkers—the goal of virtually every school in America—we have a much better chance of success if we get rid of the peculiar American notion of the lone individual clawing a path to the top and instead have students practice collaboration on a regular basis.

Is the Isolated Scholar Still Viable?

But you and I understand the problem. The typical classroom with its rows of desks facing a whiteboard does not give students much opportunity to practice collaboration. This classroom arrangement, by the way, is a direct descendant of the industrial era, when society was focused on hierarchy and survival of the fittest. The result? A recent study of 2000 U.S. schools found that students spend most of their time during the school day either listening to lectures or working individually.

Is this view of the classroom hardwired into our psyches? Of course. Take a hard look at every cartoon, advertisement, or bad movie about bad teachers. The students sit in rows; the teacher talks, or in the case of the bad movie, has horrible hair and acts like a moron.

This is another mindset issue. How do you do help break this cycle, so that decades from now, when old movies of row-based classrooms come up on the screen, viewers will shake their heads in wonderment. Here's a set of starter ideas:

- *Make collaboration the norm.* Perhaps the best thing we can do for our students is to remember that collaboration is not a soft skill. Instead, mastery of this skill should be seen as central to every young person's success. Don't be embarrassed to clearly teach to the hot intelligences by putting students in teams; assessing their communication skills; challenging them with complex, open-ended questions; and giving them the opportunity and time to go deep into issues. Speak up in favor of collaboration and teamwork at every opportunity, including global partnerships and cooperation. Don't hesitate. You will be speaking for the next generation of leaders. Start by championing a cooperative, service-oriented ethic among students, rather than a win-lose mentality. Our job, in fact, is to help young people make the world more round, and not so flat.

- *Understand that positive collaboration provokes intelligent behavior.* More people possess the key intelligences identified by psychologist as those that process "hot" information—signals concerning motives, feelings, and other domains relevant to an individual's well-being. These include personal intelligences, such as the multiple intelligences identified by Howard Gardner (1983). They also include social intelligences, the ability to interact successfully in diverse groups and situations, as well as the five intelligent behaviors—flexibility, resiliency, empathy, perseverance, and curiosity—that I've identified in this book. People high in hot intelligences know how to cooperate, act wisely in relationships, and identify the social-political dynamics of relationships. Gardner lists Socrates, Jesus, Gandhi, and Eleanor Roosevelt as people who possessed this kind of intelligence. None of them was known as a competitor.

- *Use collaboration to teach citizenship.* When Senator Bill Bradley ran for President, he wrote in his book, *The New American Story* (2007), that we need an "ethic of connectedness" to repair the rifts in American society and recapture the "can do" spirit that helped build our country. Probably no one is more concerned with the decline in civic responsibility than teachers, who are determined to graduate civic-minded young people. But it's hard to teach cooperation and a sense of the commons when the gurus of education continue to issue siren calls for a more competitive attitude among students.

- *Teach collaboration and conflict.* In an information-based world, opinions abound—and they travel fast. With so much information on hand, factions can develop and stall problems at any level—from the neighborhood to the United Nations. Finding solutions requires empathy and negotiation skills. These are not the staples of traditional education, which teaches students to be quiet until it's their turn to talk. Without practice, students will find it difficult to learn a key fact of life: conflict is inherent in collaboration. Incorporate conflict into teaching through projects that require students to work in collaborative, high-performance teams. Assess their empathy skills.

- *Use cohorts.* It's not always possible or necessary to use teams or groups. Instead, use the real-world solution that applies to nearly anyone learning today: cohorts. These are small, sometimes informal, support and feedback groups that help the individual improve their work or clarify their thinking.

- *Get out of those rows!* Rows may be great for crowd control, but they reinforce an old version of smart. Put students in circles, groups, teams, U-shapes—anything that approximates the way business operates today. Make the space in which they learn reflect the ethic we want to teach.

FROM GROUPS TO TEAMS

Finally, a few words about a step I consider critical to improving collaboration in schools: shifting our mindset from groups to teams.

In workshops, I remind teachers of the reason that the Dallas Cowboys, America's favorite football team, do not call themselves the Dallas Cowboys *group*. Groups form low-level associations for the purposes of discussion, sharing, and conferring on each other's work. Teams, on the other hand, depend on *shared intention,* which is the ability to work together for a common purpose.

Groups are central to collaboration—when we share intentionality, we identify as part of a group—but we also deliberately and explicitly agree on a goal, and can understand what others expect us to do in order to work toward the goal. Shared intentionality enables us to take collective action.

We're doing much more collaborative learning in schools, but the group work strategies of the last twenty years are aimed at cooperating, not necessarily at quality of thinking. By moving to the vocabulary of a team—a focused, committed set of individuals operating as a cohesive unit in search of a solution or attempting innovative thinking—it raises the bar by replacing the old notion of having children circle a desk and exchange information with the idea that students team for a purpose.

First, what defines a team as opposed to a group? All students understand the concept of teams, but unless they have learned from a coach who explicitly teaches the principles of teamwork, they rarely understand the deep underpinnings that make teams succeed. A good first step is to establish the difference between groups and teams. Nearly always, the differences come down to five principles that define a team. I've taken these from a previous book on project-based learning (Markham, 2012).

- *Commitment.* Teams consist of individuals committed to the success of the team, and to upholding their individual responsibilities to make the teamwork. If one individual fails to contribute, the team can fail.
- *Know their strengths and roles.* Team members know how to best contribute to a team. They know their role and obligations, as well as when and where they will likely need help.
- *Focus on a common goal.* Groups focus on process; teams focus on achievement. Teams work best when the goal is well defined and doable. All teamwork begins with the end in mind: What do we need to create, produce or achieve?
- *Ability to critique performance.* Teams practice continuous improvement by regularly reviewing objectives, measuring accomplishments, and deciding next steps. They learn from one another through objective praise and analysis.
- *Follow a process.* Teams operate by formal mechanisms and guidelines designed to foster efficiency, communication, and productivity.

Getting Started

Moving from groups to high-performing teams is a three-step process. The first step is to establish a collaborative culture by setting norms for teams and scaffolding essential skills like listening, eye contact, body posture, voice tone, and empathic responses. (These are best taught early in the year, before launching a full-scale teamwork.)

Establish the difference between groups and teams through discussion, reflection, or guest speakers from industry who can talk about the central role of teams in business. Once the discussion is over, however, you will need to consistently employ a set of tools to trains students in teamwork. This can be a lengthy, frustrating process, but teaching students to work in teams is one of the most important goals of a 21st century teacher.

Keep in mind that teams operate in stages. In early stages, they may not be effective. Give teams the time and support necessary to get better at their job, just as individuals do. When the teams begin to function at a higher level, move the bar of assessment higher.

The second step is to form your teams intentionally. Balance your teams based on individual strengths and challenges, a profile of their creativity or critical thinking skills, or their personality traits. With younger students, this works best if teachers choose team members. But older high school students can be taught how to choose their own teammates—a valuable lesson in self-awareness and self-management.

The third step is to train your teams by using team tools. Three basics tools will do the job: a high-quality collaboration rubric, a work ethic rubric, and a team contract that defines their operating agreements. (Note: I've made all of these tools available through the web; see the Afterword.)

But . . . How Do I Make Teams Really Work?

Good question, because it's not easy. Shifting to a more collaborative system of teaching and learning requires patience, skills, and technique. It's also a matter of importing ideas about teamwork from industry, which has been at this longer than education. So, more ideas here that mirror industry practices:

- *Tell students the "why" behind teams.* Share with students some of the key reasons as to why they should work in teams: motivation (many times, you can only meet your individual goals through group success); cohesion (when more than one person cares about a goal, it's easier to accomplish it); better thinking (the group mind increases mastery, finds divergent solutions, and improves critical thinking); cognitive elaboration (if you can explain it to a teammate and discuss it in depth, you understand it.); and more empathy (putting team members together forces students to know one another better, appreciate strengths and differences, and engage in growth-inducing reflection on their personal habits and personality attributes).

- *Grade teamwork.* Teamwork should not be a serendipitous by-product. You can mix and match between grading individual students in a team, overall team performance, or a mix of both, but teamwork must be graded and show up in the final unit or project evaluation—just as teams are evaluated on performance in the work world.

- *Challenge your teams.* We treat 21st century skills, such as communication and collaboration, as isolates. But at a deep level they emanate from one place—from some inner dialogue, vision, stimulation, exchange, wondering, surprise, validation, and joyful recognition of a new idea. A new idea may start with an individual, but we know they gain exponential power in the presence of a team. The kick-start for this process is an engaging, powerful challenge that liberates ideas and draws teams together for the common purpose of solving an important problem.

- *Use protocols for thinking.* A variety of tools exist to help teams learn to inquire, contribute, comment, share, respond, listen, and revise ideas. Use visible thinking tools (see Chapter 8) that force attentiveness and careful responses, or team-to-team and peer-to-peer exchanges, with a clear goal and prompts, at every opportunity. Make the students do the heavy lifting and hard thinking. Have them track and report out on their discussions.

- *Create a design mentality.* Drafting, critiquing, and revising are what teams do best. From students in teams to think in engineering terms: as designers of a prototype that needs to be reviewed and tested for quality and specifications. The product may be a written piece, a media presentation, a drawing, or a gas-powered boat. It doesn't matter. The objective is to build a culture of craftsmanship.

- *Use the power of reflection.* A reflection allows teams to probe their performance, quality of work, and overall learning. Your goal is to help the teams move through a two-stage process: From the *So what?* (What did we learn?) to the *Now what?* (How can we improve, think deeper, and move forward?).

- *Prepare for outliers.* The most common complaint about teams from teachers? "My students don't want to work together; they just want me to give them the information!" Of course. The current education system has taught students to be passive recipients of information rather than active participants. The blame lies not with the students, but with adults. We designed the system. But there are remedies. Generally, a teacher will encounter two kinds of "outliers"—those who won't work in teams or those who can't. Each requires a different approach.

- *Make the challenge authentic. Challenge* that provides the mission-critical energy that causes a team to cohere and take on a creative task with enthusiasm. In fact, there is joy in cooperative creation. Tap into that joy by matching teams to important, authentic tasks. These may be school-related, but more often they are authentic, community-oriented tasks that bring out the best in students. Really, it's a way to elicit their individual intelligent behaviors and yoke those behaviors together into a collaborative enterprise. More of this kind of learning—and less focus on one-off tests that capture little of the joy of learning—and the engagement problem would disappear.

Overall, in developing teams, take the long view. It may take an entire semester or the good part of the academic year to teach students teamwork. Remember that industry spends millions of dollars each year to train employees in this exact skill. Our goal: *every* student knows how to collaborate for a purpose by the time he or she exits secondary school. If we do that, education starts to change the world. The students will do the rest.

TEACH COLLABORATION, NOT COMPETITION

I'll end on a note of optimism and hope. I have no proof, but I believe collaborative intelligence might be nature's way of getting enough brains on the job to solve pressing global issues. If teachers foster powerful collaboration, young people will learn to work together across old borders to address fundamental issues that affect the life of the planet. Hence, the title of this section: *Teach collaboration, not competition.*

I don't mean this literally, as in give up football or spelling bees. Most students, along with adults, enjoy a contest and a challenge. But keep in mind that the origin of the English word "compete" comes from the Latin verb *competere,* which means "to come together or to strive together." All competition involves a form of collaboration—and vice versa.

Simply, I urge you to recognize that the interconnections between people go far beyond technology, and that the survivalist model of human nature as predatory and based entirely on self-interest is giving way to a newer, more informed view of humans as social creatures with natural reserves of empathy (Hanson, 2010; Olson, 2007).

This contradicts the current prevailing theory that the world is "flat"—meaning that American students need to work harder to outsmart the other players and win the race for the jobs of the future. But what if we made collaboration the norm? More importantly, what if the competitive stick is ineffective, outmoded, even self-defeating, as a means for motivating young people to learn? For one thing, international competition is the opposite of what appeals to today's youth. In all my years as an educator, I have never heard an American student express the thought, "I can't wait until I'm in the job market so I can beat the Chinese!" Yet U.S. schools, in their push for reform and performance, invoke competition and dominance on a regular basis.

In fact, studies show that this is the most intimate and connected generation of young people in history—and those connections reach beyond geographic borders. A global youth culture has emerged of individuals who share tastes in music, fashion, and lifestyle—and who also think alike. The research also shows that youth in cities as diverse as New York, Seoul, and Caracas have more in common with each other than they do with peers in their own countryside. This trend puts us squarely on the path to greater collaborative and synergistic efforts that could improve the quality of life on a global level.

Many people around the world would welcome a shift away from competition as well. Over the past two years, in addition to working with several hundred American educators, I've had the pleasure of leading workshops with teachers in Britain, Jordan, China, and Malaysia. In none of these places was competition mentioned as a key driver of educational reform or academic performance. However, a group of teachers in Beijing did stand and applaud when I mentioned the "C" word. But it wasn't *competition* that evoked their nods and smiles—the word was *cooperation.*

Of course, in all countries educators agree that schools should be graduating skillful students who can qualify for the entrepreneurial, multifaceted jobs associated with an increasingly complex global economy. But why do the skills associated with high-performance work have to focus on competition? And what if we helped young people acquire those skills by appealing to their sense of responsibility, both globally and locally? What if we tapped into the passion unleashed by service, collaboration, and contribution—a kind of "neuroscience of democracy" (Chaltain, 2014)?

This would be an enormous motivator for increasing academic performance. At this moment in history, when we could all sink together if we don't keep each other afloat, students yearn for idealism. They want a better world, and the pent-up demand for action after the last few years of drought is palpable in the world. Growing evidence suggests that students are headed toward a greater sense of service. For instance, a study released this month in California—often a bellwether for youth trends—reveals that students are not interested in winning races. Surprisingly, their goals center on home, marriage, religion, and career. In other words, they're searching for a bit of peace.

Moving Forward . . .

Extend Your Professional Network

1. ***Extend your collaboration.*** How does your professional network look? Does it extend beyond the staff room, hallway conversations, and district gatherings? No? Then the world awaits. The industry that most uses Twitter is . . . us! Sign up for a Twitter account and start hearing from educators around the globe with an infinite barrage of good news and ideas about education. And there's much more. Check the Afterword for links and sites.

2. ***Create a personalized learning ecosystem.*** This is a form of collaborative learning envisioned by educational leader Yong Zhao applies equally to students or teachers (Schwartz, 2013). Instead of relying on traditional professional development days for your growth and learning, seek out collaboration on the Internet or in other schools in your district with other teachers of like mind and goals. Share teaching and learning methods, and give each other feedback. This group becomes your personalized resource base.

Reflection Questions . . .

1. How do you coach students in groups who don't want to work with others?

2. If teams have not been successful in your classroom, why?

3. Is your classroom set up for maximum exchange and collaboration?

Afterword

Become an Agent of Change

Twelve Easy Ways to Contribute to the Conversation

I've used a large-scale lens to present ideas on redefining intelligence and inquiry-based learning, and to help forecast what I hope will become a new and dramatically improved system for youth growing up in the 21st century. But deep change will not come because of books, government mandates, pronouncements from a consortium of business leaders, or another well-funded, well-publicized study of the gaps in today's education.

The principles of inquiry and a vision of a more connected, caring, and *brilliant* system can only be fleshed out and given life through the work of teachers. Yes, details remain as to how the new world of learning will look, but you, as a teacher, play the lead role. And don't underestimate the moment. Few in history have been placed in position to contribute to such an important evolution of ideas. How do you prepare yourself for this historical opportunity?

1. Never be cynical.

It starts with attitude. Be kind, but assertive. Believe in change and progress. Get off your "buts." Even on bad days, trust that the 3 billion youth worldwide will figure out their destiny and improve the world.

2. Be autonomous.

Nothing will happen without teachers taking charge of their own destiny. The government, teacher unions, or your local elected school board may be interested in reform, but institutions move too slowly to keep pace with the tornado of change. This is a job for high-level knowledge individuals joining together in common cause and bringing about "hundredth monkey" change. Work toward professional autonomy. Know and carry out best teaching practices, but don't be a slave to the latest fad or directive.

3. Rethink scarcity.

In the networked, on-demand world, personalized learning is available to every student. There are abundant resources, courses, and helpful sites. Have a student who can't do math? Have them use the Khan Academy. This is one of hundreds of examples. Teach students to use a "click-through" mentality to develop their own program of study or supplement their course work at your school.

4. Think globally.

How long it will take to transform schools is a complete unknown. From my experience, only one thing is certain: most educators around the globe are focused on the same causes because they observe similar habits of youth worldwide. Something in the water or air or curriculum is causing them to zone out, burn out, or simply resist the conventions and traditions of normal school. A good first step is to recognize that you are not alone. Cadres of teachers in all countries share your desire for transformation and hold a keen sense of responsibility to the young generation. They understand the urgency.

A second step is to pay attention to schooling around the world. There's a tendency to become country specific, but there are advances in education throughout the world. In fact, we're beginning to learn from one another. But knowledge and responsibility must be shared, whether with colleagues in your school or across several international time zones. It's time to act.

5. Understand international trends and test results.

If you're a U.S. educator, don't let yourself feel bad because others tout Asian education or the test scores from Finland. If you're an Asian educator, don't think that the West has all the answers for creativity and innovation. Instead, let's learn from one another. Every system is trying to get better and has something to offer. One way to keep up to date? Track PISA scores and insightful commentary on international trends.

http://nces.ed.gov/surveys/pisa/

http://www.oecd.org/edu/eag.htm

6. Collaborate.

Professional collaboration is a must. Press for changes in the teaching day that allow time for conferencing and conferring with colleagues. Share teaching duties and observe colleagues. Open the door. Invite anyone into the classroom. Work hard at making Professional Learning Communities more than just a half-hearted district initiative.

7. Stay current.

Read list serves, blogs, and daily newsletters. On the recommended list for inquiry-based teachers:

http://www.mindshift.org

http://www.edutopia.org

http://www.teachthought.org

8. Bookmark the resources for deeper learning and 21st century skills.

http://dlmooc.deeper-learning.org/

http://www.p21.org/

9. Become skilled at project-based inquiry.

Project-based learning is not a fad or strategy; it's a way to implement best practices in inquiry-based education by combining intellectual rigor, intelligent behaviors, 21st century skills, visible thinking, and high-quality collaboration into one package. It allows for authentic, purposeful, real-world work by students. When done well, project-based learning just doesn't teach students; it matures them. Learn how it's done and enjoy the results. Also, look at, download, and use all the rubrics for 21st century skills mentioned in the book. Your best resources:

http://www.thommarkham.com

http://www.bie.org

10. Put positive emotions to work.

An intentional shift of focus to the physical area of the heart, along with the generation of a positive emotional state (such as care or appreciation), quickly increases heart rhythm coherence, resulting in a positive emotional shift that sharpens our thinking processes. Children and adults can easily learn this technique, and these simple heart-based tools help create learning environments that are safer, more emotionally stable, more productive and ultimately more enjoyable for teachers and students. It works.

www.heartmath.org

11. Look outside of education to learn about education.

It's amazing how disconnected education and psychology remain. Close the gap. Learn about youth development, resiliency, stress, and social-emotional learning. Keep up on basic psychological research; much of it has direct implications for educators.

http://www.casel.org/

http://www.spring.org.uk/

12. Think whole child.

You've heard enough about this throughout the book. Let go of the cognitive model and focus on bringing education back to its roots.

http://www.wholechildeducation.org/

http://www.educatethewholechild.org/what-is-it/

References

Abbott, J. (2010). *Overschooled but undereducated: How the crisis in education is jeopardizing our adolescents.* London: Continuum International.

Benard, B. (1991). *Fostering resiliency in kids: Protective factors in the family, school, and community.* Portland, OR. Western Center for Drug-Free Schools and Communities.

Benard, B. (2004). *Resiliency: What we have learned.* San Francisco, CA: WestEd.

Blad, E. (2014, April 9). More than half of students 'engaged' in school, says poll. *Education Week.* Retrieved from http://www.edweek.org/ew/articles/2014/04/09/28gallup.h33.html?r=1028329419&preview=1

Blue, L. (2012, December 26). Motivation, not IQ, matters most for learning new math skills. *Time.* Retrieved from www.healthland.time.com/2012/12/26/motivation-not-iq-matters-most-for-learning-new-math-skills/

Bradley, B. (2007). *The new American story.* New York: Random House.

Bradley, R., McCraty, R., Atkinson, M., Arguelles, L., & Rees, R. (2006). *Reducing test anxiety and improving test performance in America's schools: Results from the TestEdge national demonstration study* (HeartMath Research Center Publication No. 06-010). Boulder Creek, CA: Institute of HeartMath.

Bresser R., & Fargason, S. (2013). *Becoming scientists: Inquiry-based teaching in diverse classrooms.* Portland, ME: Stenhouse Publishers.

Bronson, P., & Merryman, A. (2010, July 10). The creativity crisis. *Newsweek.* Retrieved from http://www.newsweek.com/creativity-crisis-74665

Brooks, D. (2014, April 2). What machines can't do. *New York Times.* Retrieved April 2, 2014, from http://www.nytimes.com/2014/02/04/opinion/brooks-what-machines-can't-do

Case, R., Daniels, L. (n.d.). *Preconceptions of critical thinking.* Vancouver, B.C., Canada: Critical Thinking Consortium, University of British Columbia. Available from http://tc2.ca/pdf/profresources/Preconceptions.pdf

Chaltain, S. (2010, August 23). The science of school renewal. *Huffington Post.* Retrieved November 18, 2010, from www.huffingtonpost.com/sam-chaltain/the-science-of-school-ren_b_690031.html

Chaltain, S. (2014). The neuroscience of democracy. *Education Week.* Retrieved April 17, 2014, from http://blogs.edweek.org/edweek/civic_mission/2014/04/the_neuroscience_of_democracy.html

Clark, E. (1997). *Designing and implementing an integrated curriculum: A student-centered approach.* Brandon, VT: Holistic Education Press.

Costa, A., & Garmston, R. (2002). *Cognitive coaching: A foundation for renaissance schools.* Norwood, MA: Christopher Gordon.

Covey,. S. (2010, April 10). Our children and the crisis in education. *Huffington Post*. Retrieved on April 21, 2010, from http://www.huffingtonpost.com/stephen-r-covey/our-children-and-the-cris_b_545034.html

Cox, J. (February, 2011). *Emotional intelligence and its role in collaboration. Proceedings of American Society of Business and Behavioral Sciences, 18*(1). Available from http://asbbs.org/files/2011/ASBBS2011v1/PDF/C/CoxJ.pdf

Cozolino, L. (2012). The social brain: Why no brain heals alone. *National Institute for the Clinical Application of Behavioral Medicine Brain Series*. Webinar.

Cozolino, L. (2013). *The social neuroscience of education*. New York: W.W. Norton and Co.

Csikszentmihalyi, M. (1990). *Flow: The psychology of optimal experience*. New York: Harper & Row.

Damasio, A. (1994) *Descartes' error: Emotion, reason, and the human brain*. New York: G.P. Putnam's Sons.

Damon, W. (2008). *The path to purpose: Helping our children find their calling in life*. New York: Free Press.

Doidge, N. (2012). Unlocking the enormous potential of neuroplasticity. *National Institute for the Clinical Application of Behavioral Medicine Brain Series*. Webinar.

Dossey, L. (2010). Does technology reveal a hidden imperative toward empathy? *Huffington Post*. Retrieved May 1, 2010, from http://www.huffingtonpost.com/dr-larry-dossey/does-teachnology-reveal-a_b_557818.html?v

Dweck, C. (2008). *Mindset: The new psychology of success*. New York: Ballantine Books.

Ed pulse. (2014, January 16). *ASCD Smart Brief*. Retrieved January 16, 2014, from https://www2.smartbrief.com/servlet/ArchiveServlet?issueid=66269B00-71AD-40BA-83C6-DF84FB4D7CAB&lmid=archives

EngageNY. (n.d.). *Pedagogical shifts demanded by the Common Core*. Retrieved October 6, 2014, from file:///Users/mconnorsullivan/Downloads/common-core-shifts.pdf

Fischer, G. (2006). *Distributed intelligence: Extending the power of the unaided, individual human mind*. Retrieved May 6, 2006, from http://l3d.cs.colorado.edu/~gerhard/papers/avi-2006.pdf

Fottrell, Q. (2014, February 8). Job interviews are getting weirder. *MarketWatch*. Retrieved on February 8, 2014, from http://www.marketwatch.com/story/job-interviews-are-getting-weirder-2014-02-07

Flynn, J. (2009). *What is intelligence? Beyond the Flynn effect*. New York: Cambridge University Press.

Flynn, J. (2012). *Are we getting smarter? Rising IQ in the 21st century*. New York: Cambridge University Press.

Fredrickson, B. (2009). *Positivity: Top notch research reveals the 3 to 1 ratio that will change your life*. New York: Three Rivers Press.

Fredrickson, B., Grewen, K., Coffey, K., Algoe, S., Firestine, A., Arevalo, J., Ma, J. & Cole, S. (2013). A functional genomic perspective on human well-being. *Proceedings of the National Academy of Sciences of the United States of America,.* 110, 13684–13689.

Friedman, T. (2013, January 29). It's P.Q. and C.Q. as much as I.Q. *New York Times*. Retrieved from http://www.nytimes.com/2013/01/30/opinion/friedman-its-pq-and-cq-as-much-as-iq.html?_r=0

Friedman, T. (2014, February 23). How to get a job at Google. *New York Times.* Retrieved on February 23, 2014, from http://www.nytimes.com/2014/02/23/opinion/sunday/friedman-how-to-get-a-job-at-google.html?_r=0

Gee, J. (2003). *What video games have to teach us about learning and literacy.* New York: Palgrave Macmillan.

Gee, J. (2011, April 21). Games and learning: Teaching as design. *Huffington Post.* Retrieved from www.huffingtonpost.com/james-gee/games-and-learning-teachi_b_851581.html?vie

Gardner, H. (1983). *Frames of mind: The theory of multiple intelligences.* New York: Basic Books.

Goleman, D. (1995). *Emotional intelligence.* New York: Bantam Books.

Goleman, D. (2006). *Social intelligence.* New York: Bantam Books.

Goodman, S. (2014, March 18). Fuel creativity in the classroom with divergent thinking. *Edutopia.* Retrieved March 19, 2014, from http://www.edutopia.org/blog/fueling-creativity-through-divergent-thinking/

Hall, B. (2013, May 25). Transforming the basis of knowledge. *University World News, 273.* Retrieved from http://www.universityworldnews.com/article.php?story=20130524144726593

Hanson, R. (2009). *Buddha's brain: The practical neuroscience of happiness, love, and wisdom.* Oakland, CA: New Harbinger Publications.

Hanson, R. (2010). How did humans evolve the most loving brain on earth? *Huffington Post.* Retrieved January 3, 2011, from http://www.huffingtonpost.com/rick-hanson-phd/the-evolution-of-love_b_792668.html?vie

Hanson, R. (2012). Transforming the brain through good experiences. *National Institute for the Clinical Application of Behavioral Medicine Brain Series.* Webinar.

Hattie, J. (2009). *Visible learning.* New York: Routledge.

Heitin, L. (2014, March 5). Teachers may need to deepen assessment practices for Common Core. *Education Week.* Retrieved March 5, 2014, from http://www.edweek.org/tm/articles/2014/03/05/ndia_formativeassessment.html?qs=Teachers+may+need+to+deepen+assessment+practices+for+Common+Core

Hiam, A. (2011, February 2). How—and why—to teach innovation in our schools. *eSchool News.* Retrieved from http://www.eschoolnews.com/2011/02/01/how-and-why-to-teach-innovation-in-our-schools/

Hill, L. (2013, January 3). Job applicants' cultural fit can trump qualifications. *Bloomberg Business.* Available at http://www.bloomberg.com/bw/articles/2013-01-03/job-applicants-cultural-fit-can-trump-qualifications

Jaeggi, S., Buschkuehl, M., Jonides, J., & Perrig, W. (2008). Improving fluid intelligence with training on working memory. *Proceedings of the National Academy of Sciences of the United States of America, 105*(19), 6829–6833. doi: 10.1073/pnas.0801268105

Kaplan, K. (2013, November 19). An exciting discovery about boredom. *Los Angeles Times.* Available from http://articles.latimes.com/2013/nov/19/science/la-sci-sn-five-kinds-of-boredom-20131119

Kay, K., & Lenz, B. (n.d.). Which path for the Common Core? *EdLeader 21.* March 22, 2013. Retrieved from http://www.edleader21.com/index.php?pg=33&id=10.

Keller, T., & Pearson, G. (2012). A framework for K–12 science education: Increasing opportunities for student learning. *Technology and Engineering Teacher,. 71*(5), 12–18.

Kihlstrom, J., & Cantor, N. (2000). Social intelligence. In R. J. Sternberg (Ed.), *Handbook of intelligence* (2nd ed., pp. 359–379). Cambridge, UK: Cambridge University Press.

Kirschner, P., Sweller, J., & Clark, R. (2010, June 8). Why minimal guidance during instruction does not work: An analysis of the failure of constructivist, discovery, problem-based, experiential, and inquiry-based teaching. *Educational Psychologist, 41*(2), 75–86. Available from http://www.cogtech.usc.edu/publications/kirschner_Sweller_Clark.pdf

Kok, B., & Fredrickson, B. (2010). Upward spirals of the heart: Autonomic flexibility, as indexed by vagal tone, reciprocally and prospectively predicts positive emotions and social connectedness. *Biological Psychology, 85*(3), 432–436.

Korbey, H. (2014, February 7). Is kindergarten too young to test? *MindShift.* Retrieved February 8, 2014 from http://blogs.kqed.org/mindshift/2014/02/is-kindergarten-too-young-to-test/?utm_source=feedburner&utm_medium=email&utm_campaign=Feed%3A+kqed%2FnHAK+%28MindShift%29%202/08/2014

Leadbeater, C., & Wong, A. (2010). *Learning from extremes.* San Jose, CA: Cisco Systems, Inc. Available from http://www.cisco.com/web/about/citizenship/socio-economic/docs/LearningfromExtremes_WhitePaper.pdf

Lehrer, J. (2012). *Imagine: How creativity works.* New York: Houghton Mifflin Harcourt.

Loertscher, D., Koechlin, C., & Zwaan, S. (2009). *The big think: Nine metacognitive strategies that make the unit end just the beginning.* Salt Lake City, UT: Hi Willow Research & Publishing.

Malone, T. (2012). Collective intelligence. A conversation with Thomas W. Malone. *Edge.* Retrieved November 21, 2012, from http://edge.org.11/21/2012

Markham, T. (2012). *Project based learning design and coaching guide: Expert tools for innovation and inquiry for K–12 educators.* San Rafael, CA: Heart IQ Press.

McCraty, R. (2002). *The energetic heart: Bioelectric interactions within and between people* (HeartMath Research Center Publication No. 02-035). Boulder Creek, CA: Institute of HeartMath.

McCraty, R., Atkinson, M., Tomasino, D., & Bradley, R. (2005). The coherent heart: Heart-brain interactions, psychophysiological coherence and the emergence of system-wide order. *Integral Review, 5*(2), 10–115.

McCraty, R., & Childre, D. (2004). The grateful heart: The psychophysiology of appreciation. In R. Emmons & M. McCullough (Eds.), *The psychology of gratitude* (pp. 230–255). New York: Oxford University Press.

MindShift. (2012, September 17). *How Will Students Perform? Depends on Teachers' Expectations.* Retrieved April 17, 2014, from blogs.kqed.org/mindshift/2012/09/how-will-students-perform-depends-on-teachers-expectations/

McGonigal, J. (2012). *Reality is broken: Why games make us better and how we can change the world.* New York: Penguin.

McKibbin, M. (2014, April 24). "AP for all" works well at Grand Valley High School. *PostIndependent.* Retrieved from http://www.postindependent.com/news/rifle/11135857-113/students-frink-grand-valley

Mehta, J., & Fine, S. (2014, March 5). The importance of critical optimism. *Education Week.* Retrieved from http://blogs.edweek.org/edweek/learning_deeply/2014/03/deeper_learning_and_the_importance_of_critical_optimism_othello_not_so_much_reform_so_little_change.html?qs=Mehta+Fine

Murphy Paul, A. (2012, October 7). It's not me, it's you. *New York Times,* p. SR9.

Murphy Paul, A. (2013, September 2). Six ways to motivate students to learn. *MindShift.* Retrieved from http://blogs.kqed.org/mindshift/2013/six-ways-motivate-students-to-learn/

Newberg, A., & Waldman, M. (2012). *Words can change your brain: 12 conversation strategies to build trust, resolve conflict, and increase intimacy.* New York: Hudson Street Press.

Nisbett, R. (2010) *Intelligence and how to get it: Why schools and cultures count.* New York: W.W. Norton & Company.

Nisbett, R., Aronson, J., Blair, C., Dickens, W., Flynn, J., Halpern, D., & Turkheimer, E. (2012). Intelligence: New findings and theoretical developments. *American Psychologist, 67*(2), 130–159.

Olson, G. (2007, June 29). *Research on human nature is cause for optimism.* Retrieved June 29, 2007, from http://www.commondreams.org/views/2007/06/29/research-human-nature-cause-optimism

Palmer, P. (1998). *The courage to teach: Exploring the inner landscape of a teacher's life.* San Francisco: Jossey-Bass.

Petersen, D., & Hicks, M. (2010). *Leader as coach: Strategies for leading and coaching others.* Minneapolis, MN: Personnel Decisions International.

Peterson, C., & Seligman, M. (2004).*Character strengths and virtues: A handbook and classification.* New York: Oxford University Press.

Pillars, W. (2011, December 20). Teachers as brain-changers: Neuroscience and learning. *Education Week Teacher.* Retrieved from http://www.edweek.org/tm/articles/2011/12/20/tln_pillars.html

Pillars, W. (2012, March 27). What neuroscience tells us about deepening learning. *Education Week.* Retrieved March 27, 2012, from http://www.edweek.org/tm/articles/2012/03/27/tln_pillars_neuroscience.html?print=1

Pink, D. (2009). *Drive: The surprising truth about what motivates us.* New York: Riverhead Books.

Porges, S. (2012). Body, brain, behavior: How polyvagal theory expands our healing paradigm. *National Institute for the Clinical Application of Behavioral Medicine Brain Series.* Webinar.

Prensky, M. (2011). *The reformers are leaving our schools in the 20th century.* Available at http://www.marcprensky.com/writing/+Prensky-The_Reformers_Are_Leaving_Our_Schools_in_the_20th_Century-please_distribute_freely.pdf

Prinz, J. (2012). *Beyond human nature: How culture and experience shape our lives.* New York: Penguin.

Pruett, D. (2014, June 13). An educator's lament: Part III—Stakes of our educational demise. *Huffington Post.* Retrieved from http://www.huffingtonpost.com/dave-pruett/an-educators-lament-part-_2_b_5485782.html

Rifkin, J. (2014). *The zero marginal cost society: The internet of things, the collaborative commons, and the eclipse of capitalism.* New York: Palgrave Macmillan.

Ritchhart, R., Church, M., & Morrison, K. (2011). *Making thinking visible: How to promote engagement, understanding, and independence for all learners.* San Francisco: Jossey-Bass.

Robinson, J. (2011). *Don't miss your life: Find more joy and fulfilment now.* Hoboken, NJ: Wiley.

Rotherham, A., & Willingham, D. (2009). 21st-century skills: The challenges ahead. *Educational Leadership, 67*(1), 16–21. Retrieved from http://www.ascd.org/publications/educational-leadership/sept09/vol67/num01/21st-Century-Skills@-The-Challenges-Ahead.aspx

Rothstein, D., & Santana, L. (2011). *Make just one change: Teach students to ask their own questions.* Cambridge, MA: Harvard Education Press.

Rubin, C. (2011, October 25). The global search for education: Change leader. *Huffington Post.* Retrieved October 26, 2011, from http://www.huffingtonpost.com/c-m-rubin/michael-fullan-education-system_b_1026951.html

Salzberg, S. (1995). *Loving kindness: The revolutionary art of happiness.* Boston, MA: Shambala Publications.

Schlinger, H. (2003). The myth of intelligence. *Psychological Record, 53*(1), 15–32.

Schmoker, M. (2014, September 24). The Common Core is not ready. *Education Week.* 9/24/14. Retrieved from http://www.edweek.org/ew/articles/2014/09/24/05schmoker.h34.html

Schwartz, K. (2013, October 2). The key to empowering educators? True collaboration. *MindShift.* Retrieved October 7, 2013, from http://blogs.kqed.org/mindshift/2013/10/the-key-to-empowering-educators-true-collaboration/

Schwartz, K. (2014a, February 28). Beyond knowing facts, how do we get to a deeper level of learning? *MindShift.* Retrieved from http://blogs.kqed.org/mindshift/2014/02/how-do-we-create-rich-learning-opportunities-for-all-students

Schwartz, K. (2014b, March 12). How to teach the standards without becoming standardized. *MindShift.* Retrieved March 13, 2014, from http://blogs.kqed.org/mindshift/2014/03/how-to-teach-the-standards-without-becoming-standardized/

Schwartz, K. (2014c, January 6). The importance of low stakes student feedback *MindSet.* Retrieved January 6, 2014, from http://blogs.kqed.org/mindshift/2014/01/the-importance-of-low-stakes-student-feedback.

Schwartz, K. (2014d, April 9). More progressive ways to measure deeper level of learning. *MindShift.* Retrieved April 9, 2014, from http://blogs.kqed.org/mindshift/2014/04/more-progressive-ways-to-measure-deeper-level-of-learning/

Schwartz, K. (2014e, May 6). On the edge of chaos: Where creativity flourishes. *MindShift.* Retrieved from http://blogs.kqed.org/mindshift/2014/05/on-the-edge-of-chaos-where-creativity-flourishes/

Seligman, M. (1991). *Learned optimism.* New York: Knopf.

Senge, P. (2006). *The fifth discipline: The art and practice of the learning organization* (Rev. ed.). New York: Doubleday.

Shapiro, J. (2014). Social and emotional benefits of video games: Metacognition and relationships. *MindShift.* Retrieved May 19, 2014, from http://blogs.kqed.org/mindshift/2014/05/social-and-emotional-benefits-of-video-games-metacognition-and-relationships

Shirky, C. (2010). *Cognitive Surplus: Creativity and generosity in the connected age.* New York: Penguin.

Siegel, D. (2012). The mind lives in two places: Inside your body, embedded in the world. *National Institute for the Clinical Application of Behavioral Medicine Brain Series.* Webinar.

Siegel, D. (2013). *Brainstorm: The power and purpose of the teenage brain.* New York: Jeremy P. Tarcher.

Sternberg, R., Lautrey, L., & Lubart, T. (2003). Where are we in the field of intelligence, how did we get here, and where are we going? In R. Sternberg, L. Lautrey, & T. Lubart (Eds.), *Models of intelligence: International perspectives* (pp. 3–25). Washington, DC: American Psychological Association.

Thomas, P. L. (2010, August 9). Why Common Standards won't work. *Education Week.* Retrieved from http://www.edweek.org/ew/articles/2010/08/11/37thomas.h29.html

Tough, P. (2012). *How children succeed: Grit, curiosity, and the hidden power of character.* New York: Houghton Mifflin Harcourt.

Tschannen-Moran, B., & Tschannen-Moran, M. (2010). *Evocative coaching: Transforming schools one conversation at a time.* San Francisco, CA: Jossey-Bass.

Tugade, M., & Fredrickson, B. (2002). Positive emotions and emotional intelligence. In L. Barrett & P. Salovey (Eds.), *The wisdom of feeling: Psychological processes in emotional intelligence* (pp. 319–340). New York: The Guilford Press.

Vacharkulksemsek, T., & Fredrickson, B. (2012). Strangers in sync: Achieving embodied rapport through shared movements. *Journal of Experimental Social Psychology, 48,* 399–402.

Vaillant, G. (2008). *Spiritual evolution: A scientific defense of faith.* New York: Broadway Books.

Wagner, T. (2006, January 11). Rigor on trial. *Education Week, 25,* 28–29.

Wagner, T. (2008, October). Rigor Redefined. *Educational Leadership, 66,* 20–25.

Wagner, T. (2012a). Calling all innovators. *Educational Leadership, 69*(7), 66–69.

Wagner, T. (2012b). *Creating innovators: The making of young people who will change the world.* New York: Scribner.

Wiggins, G. (2014a, May 21). Fixing the high school—student survey, part 1 [Web log post]. Retrieved May 21, 2014, from http://grantwiggins.wordpress.com/2014/05/21/fixing-the-high-school/

Wiggins, G. (2014b, February 3). The lecture [Web log post]. Retrieved March 17, 2014, from https://grantwiggins.wordpress.com/2014/02/03/the-lecture/

Zhao, Y. (2012a, July 17). Doublethink: The creativity-testing conflict. *Education Week.* Retrieved from www.edweek.org/ew/articles/2012/07/18/36zhao_ep .h31.html?print=1

Zhao, Y. (2012b). *World class learners: Educating creative and entrepreneurial students.* Thousand Oaks, CA: Corwin.

Index

A SAGE Company

Helping educators make the greatest impact

CORWIN HAS ONE MISSION: to enhance education through intentional professional learning.

We build long-term relationships with our authors, educators, clients, and associations who partner with us to develop and continuously improve the best evidence-based practices that establish and support lifelong learning.